The 50 secrets of my success

The inspiring true story of a young multimillionaire

You can visit us at:
www.billionairerightnextdoor.com

Dany Tremblay, 1975

Success in business, Millionaire, Wealth

ISBN 978-0-9940074-1-4 (e-book English)
ISBN 978-0-9940074-3-8 (English)
ISBN 978-89436-389-8 (French)

Contents

INTRODUCTION

"I'm going to be rich!" From an early age, this was my ready response to anyone who asked: "What do you want to do with your life?" Where did I get this certainty? I haven't the slightest idea.

In our family, money was never plentiful, but neither did we lack for anything. My father and mother were not immune to financial problems. Year in and year out, like countless others, they faced some tough challenges. But one thing we always had in abundance at home was love. My parents always were – and still are – a loving, united couple, and their love certainly overflowed onto my brother and me. We were fortunate recipients, in a sense. To this day, we remain a close-knit family. This was the supreme value my parents taught us. In my mind, it is worth more than all the gold in the world. When my friends visited our home, they felt good being there and often remarked that there was a real sense of happiness in our family.

As you may have guessed from our family name (Tremblay), my mother and father came from Quebec's Lac-Saint-Jean region, a part of the country where people like to get together and celebrate. If you ask my father about his fondest childhood memories, he is most likely to recall family holiday gatherings in the Lac-Saint-Jean area (and the mountain of gifts and coats on the bed!). My mother had a wonderful career, working for more than thirty years as an elementary teacher at a school in Saint-Constant, on Montreal's South Shore. She loved what she did, but that didn't stop her from leaping at the opportunity for early retirement when the government offered it in the 1990s.

My father, meanwhile, was self-employed, working in the construction industry. Exhausted after thirty years of labor, he also opted for early retirement. Today, we can see now that they appreciate every minute of it. They enjoy a pleasant standard of living, and their finances are in better shape than ever. My father likes repeating that they're the envy of many Baby Boomers around them. Have I had something to do with this? Let's just say I haven't been completely uninvolved. I'll come back to this in the chapters that follow.

Money and finance have always been subjects of fascination for me. Even at age of six, I took more pleasure in contemplating the banknotes my uncles and aunts gave me as birthday gifts than I did in spending them. I especially loved lining them up on my bed by order of value and then admiring the scene for several minutes, marveling at the power that could come from these fabulous multi-colored pieces of paper, each with its different details according to denomination. Wow! They were really gorgeous!

I also felt a powerful attraction to coins, but I saw them more as a way of getting candy at the corner store. Of course, using the bills to feed my sweet tooth was out of the question. As a kid who collected rocks, keys, stamps and sports cards, I had already decided to collect banknotes. It was a natural reflex. When it comes to money and wealth accumulation, I was a little like the cartoon character Obelix, who fell into a magic potion when he was younger. Back then, though, I hadn't the slightest idea where this great adventure would lead me. Even today, when I look back at the last decade, I have trouble convincing myself that all this really happened. Each time I think about it, I pinch myself to see if I'm dreaming. Up to now, it has been more than a dream. Phew! I realized recently that I had what it takes to write my own story. Before that

Eureka moment, I mistakenly thought that I would have to reach the level of the Donald Trumps of this world to write a book that would interest anyone. Then, little by little, my feelings of inferiority slipped away. I recognized, thanks to comments from various people that my journey up to now had been extraordinary and my story was worth telling. At the moment I write these lines, I am thirty-six years old. My initial intention was to write one or two pages with the aim of starting this book slowly and finishing it years later. Then the words came cascading like an avalanche. The best way of knowing if you can write a book is to start with the first paragraph. In my case, it took four months to write all the chapters in this book. Never in my wildest dreams would I have thought that possible.

In the chapters that follow, you'll see that the recipe to my success is simple and can easily and endlessly be reproduced. Take full advantage: there's no patent to protect it! You'll learn how to build a financial empire, and you'll discover which traps to avoid (because I've already committed the errors for you!). You'll understand the rules governing the world of finance so that you can benefit from them. If you follow and apply these teachings, your life will be transformed beyond your fondest hopes: I assure you of this. Never forget that I began with absolutely nothing. Nobody bequeathed a fortune to me, nobody popped out of a magical hat to offer me opportunities on a silver platter. I never had advantages that others didn't – quite the opposite.

You've probably read over and over again that practically everyone who has achieved success had mentors by their side, a little like Olympic medal-winning athletes having trainers. You can rest assured that I never had one, not because I wouldn't have wanted one but simply because I didn't know anyone worthy of the label! We can all agree that a millionaire mentor who is willing and able to help us can't be found in a Cracker Jack box! Despite facing a range of obstacles, however, I managed in just a short time to build a personal fortune worth millions of dollars. The truth is clear: if I succeeded, anyone who is motivated can do the same. I know it may seem trite to say this, but there is plenty of room for tomorrow's new millionaires. I personally invite you to join the club.

The train is heading out from the station. It's up to you to embark on this great adventure. If your life isn't altogether what it should be or what you want it to be, this book may help you. However, you must be aware that you may discover you're not completely on the right track or that you're on a side road instead of the freeway. That awakening may be brutal, but it is necessary.

Last winter, while on a snowmobile ride, my brother-in-law and I ended taking the wrong trail, only noticing it fifteen minutes later. Although we had wasted some time, I told myself it could have been much worse. I was glad when we saw a sign confirming that we were heading in the wrong direction. Life is a series of learning experiences, and I feel it is important to see things in this way. Throughout the book, I'll provide you with the gift of my experience and of my many errors. I'll do this with an open heart because, above all else, I want you to succeed. And when I talk about errors, I am referring to lost time and money, which I want to help you avoid.

From now on, my mission in life is to raise my awareness to a higher level and to help people achieve fulfillment. I deeply believe that every human being who has succeeded in a given field ought to help others do the same. I personally feel this need. If I failed to accomplish this, I would have a feeling of emptiness and a sense that my mission was incomplete. Another reason driving me to write this book is my own experience as a reader. A book's weaknesses often emerge when its author has little baggage or experience to support the content. Before I begin, I would like to warn you that I do not claim to possess the absolute truth on every subject I raise. Some people will totally disagree with my views, and I respect that. Instead, you should see my journey as a true and inspiring story. The information contained in this publication consists of the author's points of view and opinions. It should in no way be interpreted as investment advice or recommendations. Each individual, based on his or her personal situation, should seek the advice of a professional before making any decision.

YOUR PRIMAL NEED/DESIRE

"A change of feeling

is a change of destiny."

Neville Goddard

Author

What drives behind the motivations that guide your life choices? Have you ever asked yourself that question? If you've never taken the time to conduct this exercise, sit back on the couch, relax and reflect on it for a few minutes. Analyze the important choices you've made over the course of your life and discover what truly motivated them. You will note that in most cases, there is a common factor behind them that constantly comes up.

Here is my **Secret Number One**: I have always known exactly what I wanted. It has been in my DNA since the very beginning. Invariably, every time I come to a crossroads in life or must make an important choice, that choice is made according to this primal need/desire, which holds sway over all others. More often than not, it is stronger than reason. For example, some people have a primal need/desire to be accepted and loved by others. By analyzing the way they act in their lives, you will discover that these people make purchases to please but, above all, to avoid displeasing others. They are virtually obsessed by what others might think. Before making a decision, they consult their close family and friends. They would never trust their own judgment in a million years.

You can surely picture the scenario. If your primal need/desire is to become a rock star, you will probably love music and play an instrument like a champ. If you have always wondered why you act in one way or another, the answer will be found in your "inner iceberg," and the specific key will be located in the part that is most deeply hidden underwater. Above all, don't bother looking in the part that is visible!

Finding your *raison d'être* or your root desire is an important step that you must clarify. And if you don't like what you find, firmly remind yourself that you have the power to change course at any time to redefine yourself. Recently, I also made this course-change in my own life. Without completely altering my foundational *raison*, let's say I somewhat toned it down. I realized that becoming rich is not an end in itself. You will most likely experience the same sensation I did when you seize upon your goal in life. Next, the first question to ask yourself is: so *now* what do I do? (with a few minutes of serious silence). I must admit to you that this blank space is somewhat nerve-wracking. In the end, the answer to this question was:

You can help others to do likewise! That answer was beyond satisfying. And so, helping people is now part of my primary mission, which is a tremendous source of motivation for me. Therefore, right off the bat, try to foresee the step that immediately follows your realization of your central Life Project.

Once you have identified your primal need/desire, you must recognize the reasons that drive you to pursue this goal. For example, if you seek to build a financial empire, you must identify the reasons why. After all, at the end of the day, what is the point of simply amassing a tremendous pile of pieces of paper? Here's my **Secret Number Two**: I know the reasons that motivate my actions. Here they are: I want to travel all over the world, whenever and wherever I want. I want to use my time as I wish and enjoy life to the fullest. I want to be free of all debt. I want to have a high standard of living, with all the advantages that entails. I want to share that with the people I love. I want to establish my own foundation to make a difference in this ol' world.

You can readily understand that without a significant amount of money, all of this is impossible. And that's why I pursue my goal. You must draw up your own similar list of reasons. Ideally, you should go to the local stationery shop to pick up a personal notebook where you can keep all your important annotations and comments. On the cover, write: My Life Project or Mission Statement, or another phrase that will inspire you. My **Secret Number Three**: I've had my own similar book for years. In fact, I have three, because I have made changes along the way. Every 6 months, I consult my Life Project notebook to see where I am and to record my progress. As a tool, it works wonderfully well. Have you ever seen a homebuilder show up on building lot without a blueprint? Or an aircraft manufacturer assembling a plane without a plan? We could rattle off similar examples ad infinitum. Planning is crucial and applies to any and all areas, even those who are building wealth. Follow this recipe to the letter, exactly the way you would with a recipe for homemade cookies. Personally, I carry out my game plan as intended, which partly explains my success.

HUMBLE BEGINNINGS

"Modesty is a species of fund

that brings its owner great interest."

Charles de Secondat

Baron de Montesquieu

The second question you have to face in order to find out if you have what it takes to become a future star of finance, or quite simply, a financially independent person, is this: What kind of relationship do you currently have with money and the accumulation of wealth in general? **Secret Number Four**: I maintain an excellent relationship with money. I respect it, and in return, money respects and appreciates me.

Québec, where I live, is something of a special case in this regard. Here, money and success are not held in high esteem; I would even say they are demonized. It's a pity, because collectively, we could do so much more if we simply changed our way of seeing things and tossed the old refrains and beliefs about money into the trash. Think about it: all the businesses here were created by entrepreneurs who sought to improve their lives. In turn, they created thousands of jobs and improved the overall condition of the community. We are talking about a virtuous circle that benefits the entire population. And so my dream for Québec is that we change our perceptions of and relationship with money, in order to harness and unleash our full potential. I sometimes find myself dreaming of what the province of Québec would look like with one or two more businesses the size and magnitude of a Bombardier.

There are a several different types of money relationships. I have listed a few below. I invite you to find the one that most closely resembles your current situation:

- The destructive relationship: members of this group love immediate gratification, because after all, life is far too short. The minute they get their hands on a twenty-dollar bill, their brains immediately set to work looking for a quick and enjoyable way to spend it. For these people, money is only good for one thing: it offers the power to consume goods and services, which in return provide a temporary sense of wellbeing. This group saves very little. And when they do, they always end up reaching into the cookie jar for all sorts of reasons. Since money is sometimes scarce, they feel an overpowering urge to indulge themselves whenever it turns up. They love to keep up appearances by driving the latest-model car whenever they can. They keep their many debts hidden. Their motto: you've got to enjoy yourself to the fullest while you're alive and spend (squander), because after all, you can't take it with you.

- The suspicious relationship: this category sees money and the accumulation of wealth as the Devil incarnate. They believe that any person who is well-off must certainly have done something a little shady. Far from daring to dream of becoming rich one day, they're convinced wealth just isn't for them. This group perfectly embodies the old saying: born with a wooden spoon in your mouth. They have few debts and are financially responsible. They have a modest lifestyle. Their favorite motto is: life is not easy… one has to be serious.

- The fear relationship: this group of people constantly fears a lack of money. They accumulate as much as they can in expectation of imminent catastrophe. Penny-pinching is second nature. They consume as little as possible and collect discount coupons by the shovel-load. Taking a risk is out of the question, and so they invest most of their savings in treasury bonds that are risk-free but generate no return, because they are convinced that they could lose everything. They rarely venture into unknown terrain. They believe ceaseless hard work is the only pathway to success. Taking more than one week of vacation per year is not an option, and anyway, it's far too expensive in the first place. Not to mention, the boss may realize that they are not, in fact, indispensible. Their favorite motto: I'm not cheap, it's just too expensive. Or: I'm not a workaholic, I love my job, and that's that!

- The "casino" relationship: this group will do anything to get to the top as swiftly as possible, even if it means cutting corners or cheating people along the way. Taking huge risks and betting everything on one shot is part of their everyday routine. They have nerves of steel and can withstand heavy losses. Of course, when things go well, they rake in juicy profits. We could even call them the "roller coaster" group. They're often knocked back to Square One but in their minds, it's only a temporary setback, and they'll make good on their losses and be flush again some day. They tend to spend extravagantly and pointlessly to show off their superiority over others. With their huge egos, they see money as a tool to proclaim to everyone that they are King of the Mountain. Their favorite motto: it takes money to make money, and if you don't have any, you are nothing.

- The healthy relationship: things are slightly different for these people. They enjoy life as others do, without falling into extravagance. They know the value of money and don't pour it down the drain. They comparison-shop before buying and often choose a year-old car over a new one. They systematically save part of what they earn and invest it for their old age. Without being cheapskates, they're always on the lookout for good opportunities. They analyze the risks and potential gain before moving forward. They are curious by nature and enjoy learning about subjects they will never master. They allow themselves to dream. Their motto: the sky's the limit. Everything is possible with effort and consistency. This group tends to gain in wealth year in and year out, whatever the economic cycle. They know where they're going and have their finances well in hand, because they prioritize progress. Their motto: this little seed will grow into a big, strong tree in a few years. Other types of relationships exist, but you know what I'm talking about. Which category do you find yourself in right now? If you find yourself in any category other than this last one, your chances of becoming rich or <u>permanently</u> financially independent are slim.

The good news is that if this potential for failure makes you more uneasy than does staying where you are right now, then you have the potential to change your trajectory. It's up to you to decide, since no one will do it for you. You are where you are today as a result of thousands of decisions you've made since your birth, like a mathematical equation that successively adds up to produce the current final result. The same is true for what follows next. Most people have an array of reasons to justify their failure. You probably do not want to be a member of that group. Like most people, I had very humble beginnings. As a 10-year-old, I was a good student, above average in student performance, although not head of the class. I had a certain talent for learning without expending too much effort. Sports offered me the greatest opportunity to develop self-confidence. No matter the sport, I knew that I could perform well with a little perseverance. And I definitely enjoyed winning above all. Nothing motivated me like beating the best. And when I lost, I didn't make a big deal out of it. I simply came back stronger in the next game. On the financial level, I did pretty well for a kid my age, with a total estimated fortune of about $400! The beauty of living with your parents is that you have almost no expenses. And smartphones didn't exist back then... I also had the opportunity to develop a mini-business at home – I was my dad's banker! Sometimes, he would run short on pocket money by the end of the week. I much preferred to keep my money in hand, but since he needed it, he always managed to convince me by promising to repay the amount with interest a few days later. Thus, a loan of $40 was returned with $5 in interest on top of the capital. Not a bad return. I can already hear readers cry foul here (honestly, doing that to your own father...). But keep in mind that he was the one who solicited my services as a lender, and that he was happy to pay me back with interest. Personally, I far preferred to leave my money in peace, but that was not always possible. You can ask him today if my decision to make an exception was helpful.

I'd also heard that my brother was considerably more usurious than I was when it came to interest. I suppose that's why my father tended to come to me... At the time, I had one sole vice: I loved videogames. Strangely, Nintendo games were more expensive when I was young than they are now, making them just about the only thing that hasn't gone up over time. So it was a sizeable expense but what can you do, youth must be lived and I was no different from other young people in that respect.

Things really started rolling when I was 14. After a series of arguments, my parents gave in to the pressure and bought me a scooter. The cleverest trick I used to convince them was telling them that I could find a student job if I could get around. Through ceaseless repetition of the message (the trick used by every kid), they finally cracked. However, once I had my scooter, I kept my word by offering my services as a dishwasher in a French restaurant. In order to land the job, I went straight to the head chef, who strangely resembled the one in the film "Ratatouille." I don't know why, but he gave my chance.

Shortly thereafter, I crossed over to the other side of restaurant, into the dining room, where I worked as a busboy. I'm glad I fell into the restaurant business, because I worked in it throughout my studies. You either love the restaurant business or you don't. There is no grey area. I loved being among the clientele, because it was impossible to get bored. Time passed very quickly and I soon became addicted to the adrenaline pumped out by jam-packed dining rooms and endless waiting lines of clients.

Towards the end of my studies, I hit the jackpot (you can say that again) by landing a position as busboy in the V.I.P. salon of the Casino de Montréal. For those who have not heard of this section, it's an exclusive salon featuring a buffet where everything is free: food, alcohol, cigarettes. It is aimed at high rollers. I always enjoyed telling clients in the salon that I would inevitably win at gambling... but only once every 2 weeks, when I got paid! It should be noted that casino employees are not permitted to gamble in any casino in the province. And as far as I'm concerned, that's a very good thing. I truly enjoyed the 2 years I spent working in that establishment. First of all, I had been chosen from among thousands of candidates. Second, at the age of 18, I was the only member of my age group of friends and acquaintances be earning that much money, and relatively easily at that.

PREDESTINATED BEHAVIOR .20

PREDESTINATED BEHAVIOR

"Those who master themselves and their behavior

can change their lives."

Anthony Robbins

Author and motivational speaker

You're probably wondering what it was about me between the ages of 10 and 20 that predestined me to become the person I am now. I would answer: a number of small factors. Here is my **Secret Number Five**: as a general rule, I did not enjoy spending money in silly ways. Given that I worked at night as a dishwasher and then as a busboy on weekends, I couldn't spend my money in bars the way my friends did. Instead, I was earning money.

In your life, do you reflexively, systematically set aside part of your income aside to safeguard it? Be honest: when it comes to consumer habits, are you the kind of person with a collection of 100 pairs of shoes in the closet? Never forget that the value of all consumer products you'll find in a boutique falls to $0, or very close to that, the second you walk out the door of the store. That's not really the strategy of the century if you want to become financially independent...Back then, when I received my paycheck, I made it my duty to use my school lunch hour to head to the bank and deposit it all. I would tell myself that the higher that amount got, the better chance I'd have to buy something truly worthwhile. After a year of hard work I had eventually accumulated the princely sum of $4,000. Don't forget that I was working for $5 an hour in the 1980s and 1990s. I was very strongly tempted to trade up from the scooter to a car. And so I acquired my first vehicle. The timing was perfect, because at 16, I had just earned my driver's license. It was a superb Volkswagen Golf cabriolet, aqua green. I probably don't need to tell you that this car made me a star at my school. However, little did I know back then that the hardest experience I'd ever endured was just around the corner.

One fine morning a year after buying my car, while I was on my way to school, a police officer pulled me over for a routine check. After a long wait, I began to wonder what was going on. The police officer checked out and compared serial numbers all over the vehicle. Many long minutes later, the officer announced that he was going to search my vehicle because he suspected that my Volkswagen was a stolen car that had subsequently been made over.

Stunned, I told him to check my papers, because they were in perfectly good order. The officer then informed me that I had most likely been the victim of fraud, and for that matter, not the only one. After about 5 hours of questioning at the police station, I was set free without any criminal charges, but likewise without a car – and in a state of shock. A few weeks later, the verdict came down. It was indeed a stolen car that had been made over. After going over information on previous owners with a fine-toothed comb, the police uncovered the guilty parties. It was a body shop that specialized in this type of fraud. This, unfortunately, did not make my vehicle reappear. It was a hard life-lesson. I had to start over virtually from scratch. I had lost an entire year of income from my hard work. I was devastated.

My mother consoled me by saying that, after all, it was only one year's work in a lifetime, and that I would soon get over it. Today, I can easily say that she was right. At that moment, however, I was far from convinced. Have you ever felt like the sky had fallen on you? My **Secret Number Six**: learn lessons from hardship. I believe it is most important to learn them for next time – because there is always a next time. I personally believe that God sends us similar circumstances later in life simply to see if we've learned our lesson well. The experience taught me to be wary, to conduct more research, and to be less impulsive in my choices. When an opportunity seems too good to be true, that's because it is. I had paid $4000 for the car, but the police informed me that it had a market value closer to $10,000$. That was probably why I'd been so successful with it!

I dedicated the weeks that followed to looking for a new vehicle. A few weeks later, I found a car that was less glamorous but fun to drive. It was a 5-year-old Honda Civic. The seller had been the sole owner. There was no danger of it having been stolen. What's more, it was in good condition. The problem was that I didn't have the full amount required to purchase the car. I was exactly $5000 short. My mother therefore suggested that I obtain a bank loan with her as guarantor. Long live mothers!

I was once again the proud owner of a car, with the added gift of a loan on my shoulders. And the moment I received my first bank statement, I swiftly realized that the roles had been reversed. I was no longer the banker as I had been with my father in the olden days. I had effectively taken on the role of borrower, a situation I did not like in the slightest from the very first… especially when I discovered the amount the bank would extract from me every month. I must add that, back then, interest rates were very steep. Being a slave to the bank any longer was out of the question. My **Secret Number Seven**: I hate consumer debt. I decided then and there to work all summer to rid myself of this financial burden. Every time a fellow employee wanted time off, I made myself available. I worked very hard, but it as worth it. By September, my loan had been completely paid off. Two and a half years before the end of the contracted term. I calculated that, in making all those small sacrifices, I had deprived the bank of $1300 in interest, to my benefit – a decent amount for a student who was working for minimum wage. Do you make the sacrifices necessary to make your dreams come true? Do you consistently try to limit interest charges on your bank loans? I strongly encourage you to adopt this behavior, because it is undeniable that interest charges harm your standard of living.

EMPLOYEE OR ENTREPRENEUR?

"Nothing ventured, nothing gained."

Michel Tremblay

My dad

Having lived with one wage-earning parent one parent-entrepreneur, I was privileged from an early age to be able to compare both sides of the coin. As a teacher, my mother enjoyed a guaranteed job and salary, as well as two months of vacation every year. To me, that seemed like a dream job. As for my father, he had his own construction business. He experienced periods when work was plentiful and profitable, and also leaner times when things were difficult. I witnessed frustrating situations when he would have difficulty collecting the money due him, even though the work had been done well.

One day, when I was 12, I asked him why he had made that choice. I found that my mother was in an enviable, risk-free position. He responded that in life, "nothing ventured, nothing gained." I would only understand the meaning of that response several years later.

You're probably wondering where he got that saying. The answer is simple: straight from his own father who is, of course, my Grandpa Tremblay. Unfortunately, I never knew him, because he had passed away long before I was born. However, I had often heard him mentioned, because he was an entrepreneurial living legend. In fact, he had been the biggest general contractor in the Lac St-Jean region. I often ask people who knew him to tell me about him, because I have the impression that he's still with us, watching over me, and I want to honor his memory. According to the people who knew him, he was a convivial person who dearly loved his peers, his family and his employees. Every Christmas, he would receive a mountain of gifts from his employees, who greatly appreciated him. I can tell you in all honesty that my Grandpa Tremblay lives on in my heart, and that I hope he is proud of me. He was responsible for building the Alma Hospital, bridges and roads, schools, etc…he didn't miss a thing. Today, I know that I take after my grandfather quite a bit, and I still draw inspiration from him. However, back when I was 12, I had made my own choice. I wanted to become a salaried employee one day rather than an entrepreneur, influenced as I was by the income security factor.

I will always remember receiving my first paycheck as a dishwasher in restaurant Le Crocodile on Montreal's South Shore. I had calculated that 80 hours of tireless work at $5 an hour would put $400 in my pockets. Looking at the check, I was amazed to discover that a considerable amount was missing. Before going to see my boss, I asked a colleague if he could help me understand what had happened. He immediately answered that the missing amount represented the taxes that the government had deducted at source. "Welcome to Québec, and get used to it, because that's the way it's going to be for the rest of your life," was what he told me. I could not believe it – nobody had informed me that in addition to working for yourself, you had to work for the government. I was deeply frustrated by the situation. By the same token, I understood that I would have to go to school in order to earn a much higher salary, because one now had to live with the implacable reality of working for three entities: the provincial government, the federal government, and, finally... myself. My dream of becoming rich looked like it was going to be much more difficult than expected.

GOING TO SCHOOL FOR BETTER RESULTS AND A DIPLOMA.

"Remain seated upon a rock for three years if necessary,

because perseverance is always rewarded."

St. Paul of Tarsus

Founder of Christianity

you possibly can and earn a degree in order to land a good You've certainly heard this maxim time and time again in your life: it's very important to go to school. Go as far as job and a good salary. We become so conditioned by this type of phrase, and I did exactly that. At the age of 18, I enrolled in school to become a mechanical engineering technician. The program consisted of three years of specialized study, which I found tiresome and interminable. Furthermore, a fourth year was required to fulfill certain course requirements that I had failed during the program.

These years of study put my patience severely to the test. The most important thing to me was to finish as quickly as possible and earn my degree. Many students dropped out along the way. My **Secret Number Eight**: I do not give up easily. Quitting was not an option for me. Job prospects were excellent in that field and I intended to get my slice of the pie. When I earned my diploma, luck smiled upon me for a second time. I was immediately hired as a draftsman for an aeronautics firm. My salary was slightly lower than what I'd earned at the Casino de Montréal but as far as I was concerned, the priority was gaining experience linked to my area of study. Just to be on the safe side, I had decided to take a sabbatical year from the casino in case my new job did not suit me.

If you asked me today for my general thoughts on school, I would answer that genuine life experience is by far the most important factor in success. Think about it: what percentage of what is learned in the classroom do we really use in our professional lives? Personally, I think that it's no more than 10%. And the elements essential to becoming financially independent simply are not in the school curriculum. That must be the reason that the most intelligent people I've known in my life are not the ones who have performed best financially. On the other hand, my studies enabled me to land a job that made me a citizen of the middle class, and from that moment, I truly began to build wealth. In all, I landed three jobs in my field of study in five years. And each time, I left for a higher salary. I bought my first house at the tender age of 21. At the time, I was working for American aeronautics multinational Pratt & Whitney. I was still living with my parents, given all it cost me was a nominal rent of $100 per month! On an annual salary of $38,000, my savings rate was practically 50% of my net salary.

My **Secret Number Nine**: I have always saved systematically. Things were going well for me. However, at that moment, the picture was not as rosy for my parents. My father had spent two years executing a series of renovation contracts in partnership with a certain "Uncle" whom I naturally nicknamed: "Uncle Bastard." The problem was that my father had been paying himself a minimum wage salary in order to reinvest the profits into the company to promote its growth. His greatest mistake was in not keeping an eye on company finances.

The profits accumulated nicely, all right, but they ended up in the pockets of Uncle B., who vanished into thin air. In addition to defrauding the company, he had left another lovely gift for my parents: a spectacular unpaid line of credit of $50,000, for which they were listed as guarantors. I still recall that it was the equivalent of a 10-year financial setback for them. The problem was that they were already entering their fifties. My poor father was completely devastated. I remember that year that his hair turned white practically overnight. And so my parents suggested that I buy the family home at very favorable terms in order to reimburse the infamous line of credit, and so they could retire in peace to their summer home in the Laurentians. For me, this meant acquiring a house without having to pay a penny as down payment. Moreover, my father had built the house at a cost price of $70,000, and so that was the sales price we agreed upon. Of course, the potential resale value was much higher. With my father's misfortune, I learned a lesson that has served me well to the present day. My **Secret Number Ten**: never, never, never put blind faith in people in matters of money.

THE YEARS PASS

"They always say time changes things, but you actually have to change them yourself."

Andy Warhol

Artist

At 25, my small personal fortune had reached $35,000, with about an additional $15,000 in equity on my property. My **Secret Number Eleven**: always maintain a standard of living below what you can afford. By standard of living "below," I mean living at 85% of my financial capacity. That remains the case today, with the remaining 15% mainly directed into a registered retirement savings plan (RRSP) to take advantage of the available tax shelter.

Using 85% of my salary, I still managed to enjoyed life as much as anyone else did, even though I had to bear the burden of a house by myself. The indispensible tool was having created a budget, followed to the letter. In the "discretionary spending" column, (restaurants, outings etc...). I had written: $120 per week, and no more.

The other decisive factor involves credit cards. Here is my **Secret Number Twelve**: I have never paid a cent in interest on an unpaid balance. I have always had an automated payment in place to pay off the monthly balance on the card (the total balance, not the minimum balance payment). Also, I used one card, not ten of them! At an average of 18% on unpaid balances, it is easy to understand that this is a trap to be avoided at all costs. However, one in two folks only pays the minimum balance every month! It's a disaster for the cardholder, who is caught in a diabolical spiral of debt, and a gold mine for the card-issuing banks. Some people might wonder why I had a credit card at the age of 18. My response: for the sake of simplicity, not to consume more. A dollar spent on my card or in cash always represented the same value in my budget.

The other decisive factor was my car (the Honda Civic). You will remember that I had managed to completely pay it off during a single summer (3 months). My **Secret Number Thirteen**: keep your car for at least eight years. During that time period, I did not incur a single payment or debt on my vehicle, which enabled me to more quickly build up my savings. I resisted the temptation to replace my car with a newer model, even if I had the means to do so. When I compared the two ideas side to side, the paid-for debt-free car always won out. Making major efforts in the short term to produce major benefits in the long term has always been a component of my way of thinking. This has guided my actions and decisions for many years. Most people do exactly the opposite. They want to enjoy absolutely everything right now and on credit, even though they are well aware that it will be harmful in the long term. There are two fables that wonderfully explain the concept and my ideas on the subject: the Ant and the Grasshopper, and the Tortoise and the Hare. In the respective cases, strive to become the Ant and the Tortoise, because eventually, they are the ones who win.

THE MONT-TREMBLANT PROJECT

"Ninety percent of millionaires

became so through owning real estate."

Andrew Carnegie

Steel magnate

Are you the type of person who likes to own real estate? If you answered *yes*, then welcome to the club. I will return to this subject in-depth later in the book. This chapter is included because it had a tremendous effect in our lives over the years that followed. It demonstrates how a simple choice can have a significant impact on the events that follow. When I turned 22 in the 1990s, the economy in general in Québec was moribund. The only place where there seemed to be construction cranes was Mont-Tremblant in the Laurentians. For my part, I was working in aeronautics, a sector that was doing well at the time. Things were different for my father, because work was hard to find. That's when he discovered the region, where he was delighted to find work quickly.

The problem was transportation. The daily commute from his house in the Laurentians was 2 hours and 30 minutes. Exhausted by this rigmarole after 6 months, he resigned himself to renting a room weekly in a shabby little house with many other working tenants like himself. With its paper-thin walls, privacy was non-existent, according to him. It must be understood that in general, the life of a construction worker is no fairy tale. My father seemed to be the only person there who lived a normal life.

Soon finding it impossible to live among those people, he began talking to my brother and me about the possibilities of investing in a piece of property in Mont-Tremblant. Our curiosity piqued, we decided to organize a family visit to explore what the region had to offer. Right off the bat, we fell in love with the mountain and the real estate projects being built by the Intrawest company. They used every marketing trick in the book to sell us the dream of becoming the privileged owners of property at the foot of the mountain, right in the heart of the action.

That very same day, my brother, my parents and I completed an offer to purchase a new condo unit. Construction of the project was underway – in fact, my father was working on it, tinting all the doors on the property. He liked to say that he would be tinting the door of our future family unit. Prospectus in hand, the family delegated me with the task of analyzing all the details of the investment. It was a one-bedroom condo. The price was $115,000, plus taxes. It was a large sum for the time, considering the size.

After analyzing the prospectus, I had to admit to the others that the rental scenarios and expectations had been aggressive and probably exaggerated. In order to make the investment profitable (positive cash flow) our unit would have to be rented out 85% of the time throughout the year – a virtually unattainable ratio considering the fact that some seasons were less popular with tourists than others (for example, the months when there is no skiing). Furthermore, if my father lived in the unit, according to his original idea, the mortgage fees and common costs would make the total bill too costly. The final family decision was to cancel the purchase offer. Our dream had gone up in smoke. We were all a little sad to crash back down to earth so brutally. The reality was painful... but life still had a lovely surprise in store for us.

Two months later, our father called my brother and me a second time. This time, the situation was slightly different. it was a one-bedroom condo, similar to the previous one. The difference lay in the fact that it was not located at the foot of the mountain. It was instead located in Tremblant Village, several kilometers away. The condo was part of a 25-year-old building complex that had been neglected over the years. On the other hand, the condo was priced at $44,000, which most filled my father with enthusiasm. He endlessly repeated that there wasn't a better price in town, and that we could enjoy the same privileges we would have at the foot of Tremblant. In addition, he could live there economically and luxuriously, certainly compared to the room he was then in. After visiting the unit, our misgivings were confirmed. There was no glamor to speak of – to say the least. A little discouraged, we reluctantly made a purchase offer of $40,000. It was accepted as is, and so shortly thereafter, we had become the proud owners of a condo in Mont-Tremblant. Financed with a mortgage to the tune of 80%, we each had to contribute $4000 for a down payment, which was reasonable. When my father stayed there, he used his free time to renovate, pleasantly transforming the interior appearance and enhancing the value of our condo. Two months later, we received a letter inviting all owners to an annual meeting. When the day arrived, my brother and I happened to be at our parents' home in the Laurentians. Having nothing particular in our agenda that day, we decided on an impulse to jump into his car and head to Mont-Tremblant.

During the meeting, the Council informed us of the problems and challenges of co-ownership in their context, and there were many. As the meeting ended, they informed us that all the members of the Council were resigning, and would therefore not run for a second mandate. A vote was required to elect the new members of the council. **Secret Number Fourteen**: seize opportunities quickly when they present themselves. That was when I lowered my voice and told my brother that I would be interested in a position. Smiling broadly, he immediately took me at my word and raised his hand to advance my name. Another person in the room seconded my candidacy. Everything was approved in the minutes that followed. And that is how, at the age of 22, I took up a position managing a co-ownership property with approximately 125 units! It was decided with the other three board members of the council that I would occupy the role of treasurer. What a happy coincidence! In all, I sat for two mandates on the board of directors of the co-ownership property, and I can tell you things got pretty feisty in there, albeit in a good way.

In just one year, the co-ownership association finances went from negative to positive. In all, $18,000 of the unpaid line of credit was fully reimbursed. It was unheard of. In addition, our team moved forward with more aesthetic improvements to the complex than in the previous 25 years. In one of the major improvements, we refreshed the exteriors of all the buildings and brought them up to date, because they bore the colors they'd had since the very first paint job.

I personally participated in the bidding process for the exterior work. Naturally, my father wanted a shot at the opportunity. Among the three businesses submitting bids, my father's was the lowest, at $15,000. He therefore automatically won the bid. I knew from that minute that the work would be done extremely well. He calculated that after the costs of manpower and material, he would retain about $30,000 in profit following the completion of the work. He poured his heart into the project, and the result was worth the effort, thanks in part to my mother's involvement. And the projected profits materialized as expected. I was very happy to have helped my parents get the contract because it partially compensated them for the misfortune experienced with "Uncle."

The condo in Tremblant was a good investment. When my father was absent on weekends, it was could be rented out. We kept the condo for four years in all. Given its low purchase price, we were always able to cover all of our fees and then some with the rental income – which wasn't the case for the owners of high-priced condos at the foot of the mountain. We had, in a way, enjoyed our condo free of charge. And on resale we accepted a price of $60,000.

Our money had done its work very well: $20,000 in profit with an initial down payment of $12,000 equals a return of 166%. **Secret Number Fifteen**: stay well away from investment products presented with pretty brochures and videos. More often than not, the price will be inflated as a result. Had we chosen the nice condo at the foot of the slopes, my father would not have landed the tinting contract for the buildings. And that would have had a major impact on our future projects. The choice, and that dose of humility served us very well in the events to follow.

WANTING MORE

"Think big"

Donald Trump

Real estate billionaire

Did you know that the vast majority of people – I would say 95% – seek out a stable career offering security and a couple of weeks of vacation per year? The type of job where you know in advance what you'll be doing during the day, including when work begins and when it ends (the famous "9 to 5"). This group likes to know in advance what they will earn during the month and hopes that this everyday routine will take them straight to a golden retirement. I respect this worker's mindset and the values that accompany it. I must, however, lay down a caveat regarding the false sense of security that surrounds high-paying jobs. Throughout my lifetime, I've constantly seen and heard news reports about people who spent 20 years or more working for a business that closed down, that outsourced or relocated jobs, or suffered deep job cuts. Even the supposedly protected public sector was recently shaken up at the federal level in 2012 with drastic job cuts intended to re-establish a balanced budget. The post office has been the victim of changing technology, especially due to the Internet, which has made the traditional "snail mail" letter practically obsolete, something right out of the dinosaur era. Is that what you call security? I would instead describe that as tremendously risky. Today, security is a huge myth invented by the Baby Boomers, rather than a reality. I had clearly decided that I would not fall victim to this false concept. Are you among those who seek out job security above all else? If you answered in the affirmative, at the very least, be aware of the realities of today's world.

Thankfully, the decisions I'd made between the ages of 18 and 25 were about to catapult me to a higher level. I didn't know it at the time, but a major turning point was around the corner. It is very important to note that had I not acted as I had in the preceding years, I would not have been financially ready to embark upon the adventure I set out upon in 2001.

At 19, I signed on for a permanent subscription to business magazine. I had always been very interested in the business world. This magazine has a wide variety of articles, addressing both local and international stories; every week, it allowed me to plunge into the worlds of investment and entrepreneurship that fascinated me. My **Secret Number Sixteen**: always seek to learn something new. Reading the articles, I quickly recognized that successful entrepreneurs seemed truly accomplished, proud and happy with what they'd done for their businesses. I genuinely admired them, even more so when I realized the annual sales turnover of the companies they managed. It became evident that they had a standard living much higher than a salaried employee.

However, it was thanks to the series of cumulative small daily actions over the course of my 7 years as a salaried employee, that I had gotten as far as I had. They had made the difference in what would become the next chapter of my life. Without them, nothing would have happened, and that must not be forgotten. At 25, I had achieved an enviable track record for someone my age. There was just one cloud on the horizon: I had felt for some time that the path I took every day was simply too slow. For example, with earnings of $52,000 per year, after taxes payroll deductions had been taken, there was just over $30,000 left in my pockets. After annual expenses had been taken into account, my personal wealth increased every year by between $6000 and $8000. Realizing my dream of becoming rich seemed out of reach if I continued along the same path.

Additionally, I was no longer satisfied being an employee. The routine became boring and I felt like a robot waiting for lunchtime and the end of the workday. It was clear in my head that I would never reach my full potential in this manner. I had the feeling that all this was not meant to last much longer. The desire to be my own boss was growing stronger and stronger. That's when I was reminded of my father's famous phrase…"nothing ventured, nothing gained." And he was absolutely right. For me, being a salaried employee would be like saying: I am satisfied with not having much, because I love my comfort zone, and I don't want to lose what I've acquired, which was hard-won. I understood its full meaning at that moment. I could easily have remained in that comfort zone, which would have fossilized me with the passing years. I knew that my true path was elsewhere, and that I must find it at any cost. From that moment, I made it a habit to keep my eyes wide open in case a great business opportunity presented itself.

DRIVE FORWARD, GET AHEAD

"All life is an experiment. The more

experiments you make, the better."

Ralph Waldo Emerson

American philosopher and poet

Step by step, I made headway with my idea of becoming an entrepreneur. At first, I went to the newsstand to find publications specializing in franchises. A franchise seemed perfectly suitable to me. Buy an already established name to launch oneself into business, thereby reducing the risks: that seemed like the ideal recipe. Given I had no real experience in business, I could count on the support of the franchiser. There was no lack of choices, with plenty of options, and I just had to pick the right one.

The restaurant business was my preferred choice. To be honest, I loved and missed working in it. And so I was certain that it was the perfect option. It wouldn't be work to me; rather, it would be time invested in reaching my full potential. I just needed to find the perfect flag to fly under. Strangely, only one had managed to truly hold my attention during the selection process. At the time, I was not overly worried about the amount I would have to provide as a down payment to secure the franchise. I simply told myself that I would find a way to cross that bridge when I got to it…

That was the moment I took the first step that most people never take. **Secret Number Seventeen**: act, without passively waiting for things to happen by magic. I grabbed the telephone called the head office. They gently requested some personal information and responded that a formal application would be mailed to me within a week. Wow: I felt butterflies and a sense of lightness right then and there, as I had realized that something extraordinary might genuinely come of this. I had set the train in motion and it would take me to my destination.

With my momentum in full gear, I headed to the Government of Canada website that very day to inform myself on the procedure for incorporating a new business. To my considerable amazement, the process was very simple and quick. In under an hour, I had my certificate printed out confirming that as of October 10, 2000, the business was registered. The official paperwork would be mailed out several days later. Once again – wow! My business had been born. I was genuinely proud of myself that day, because I had the impression that I had made the necessary commitments and taken the first steps in the right direction. An adventure in its embryonic stage had begun. I was now eager to see how events would unfold and to find out what life had in store for me.

That weekend, my spouse and I went to our condo in the Laurentians to go cycling and enjoy nature at Mont-Tremblant. On the return trip to Montréal, we were in Laval on Highway 13, just before crossing the bridge into Montréal. I spontaneously pointed towards a un site en bordure de the highway and said to her: I think that a restaurant…(in X chain) would work very well if it were located here. She immediately answered "yes." Her show of interest pushed me to pursue my line of thought.

I asked her if she would quit her job to leap into this adventure. She burst into laughter and answered me ironically: "Oh yeah, of course, I will quit my job as a supervisor at Lise Watier to sell donuts." I sat there with my jaw hanging open. Consequently, I deliberately avoided mentioning the discussion I'd had with the employee of the parent company several days earlier. In the course of this book, I will intentionally avoid mentioning the name of chain in question. Why? We still have legal agreements with the parent company that remain in force today.

BEING ON THE RIGHT TRACK

"I always knew I was destined for greatness."

Oprah Winfrey

TV host, Producer

Do you occasionally daydream about what your life would be like with unlimited wealth? What would you do with your days? Would you golf every day, or linger in your garden? I've noticed that the wealthiest people are those who work a lot and have packed schedules and very busy lives. They do what they are most passionate about, because sitting around doing nothing – even with all the money in the world – isn't very exciting.

Several weeks passed without anything in particular happening. I received my request forms as expected and as soon as I had, completed and returned them to the consignee. I did not hesitate because I had followed up on the subject with my wife, revealing the entire process involving the parent company. She had then revised her position, stating that after all, she would take on the position of boss, which was an enviable one indeed. I had filled out a second request with another chain that seemed a less interesting prospect. Quite simply, I wanted to increase my chances of success. The following week I received a phone call at work from my first choice. It was the head of development, who asked me if I was still interested in a franchise. I answered yes. She immediately pursued the issue, asking if my wife and I were ready to give up everything else to devote ourselves exclusively to the chain. I again answered yes, although I was a little nervous answering on my wife's behalf. She continued questioning me on my availability for an interview. The date was set for the following evening in their offices.

Secret Number Eighteen: you must know how to make a sales pitch to achieve what you desire. The following evening, the interview was indeed held at the appointed time and place. The atmosphere was relaxed, with a vibrant energy. Both sides had plenty of questions, and after all was said and done, we had the impression that it had gone well. Right from the start, it as made clear that in this business, you had to roll up your sleeves and put in long hours. Training took place in Ontario and would stretch out over a two-month period before the opening of the restaurant. I then asked if, by chance, we had been designated with the location along Highway 13 in Laval. As if by magic, the woman smiled and seemed slightly surprised to hear the question, as though I had already been informed, answered that we had. It was surreal. I was completely stunned. She mentioned that there were other sites available. We responded that the Laval option remained our number one choice.

At work the following day, after lunch, there was a message in my voicemail. It was the head of development, congratulating me and my wife. We had been chosen, and were now part of the big family. She also mentioned that we had been granted our first restaurant location choice. We would have to quit our jobs within a maximum of two weeks. Our training was urgent and would begin in the first week of December with the planned official opening of the restaurant set for February 4, 2001. At that moment, I understood that events can unfold quickly when we set things in motion.

My life was going to change completely if the project became a reality. Also, at only 25, I would become the youngest franchisee of the restaurant chain in the country.

PITFALLS

"It is never crowded along the extra mile."

Wayne Dyer

Author

Are you still there? Good, because I've got to clarify an important point. My question is as follows: did you purchase this book hoping to find a magic formula that would make you rich overnight without any effort? If you answered *yes*, then I must be honest and tell you that you've made a mistake. I want to warn you about people in this world with ill intentions who loudly proclaim that you can get rich quickly and easily.

I personally know of no way to do so. For that matter, our sense of logic repeatedly tells us: if it were that easy, everybody would be doing it. Have you ever had a brilliant idea worth millions of dollars only to subsequently learn that the road to realizing that goal is strewn with pitfalls? We were no exception to that rule, as our journey proves. Obviously, any large-scale project entails its own set of challenges to be met, and our list on that score was fairly long. Undeniably, the biggest challenge was financing. The total cost of the franchise was $390,000. Securing the bank loan required a personal down payment of 25%. A further $25,000 in net working capital was needed to begin commercial activity.

We did not have the entire sum at our disposal. At the time, our savings amounted to $35,000, plus $15,000 in equity on the family home, which had been rented out to a third party for a year. Therefore, including the net working capital, we were missing $75,000 – an amount high enough to discourage many. **Secret Number Nineteen**: you must be extremely creative when it comes to finding financing for a business. In order to get there, we decided to take things step-by-step. I came up with the idea of using my good credit rating to open a personal line of credit of $15,000. Given that the business loan was being worked out with the Royal Bank, I intentionally made my request for a line of credit with the Caisse Populaire.

I fell upon an incredible stroke of luck. At the Caisse, I bumped into an employee who turned out to be a friend from high school. She granted my line of credit without a problem. I hadn't known she was working there, because we'd lost sight of one another after school ended. Asking me what I planned to use my line of credit for, I answered that Chantal and I wanted to get married and enjoy our honeymoon on credit! It wasn't entirely untrue, since we would indeed get married a year later… but certainly not on credit! In any case, admitting to her that we planned to quit our jobs and start a business was out of the question. Even though she was my friend, our true risk profile would have taken precedence, to the detriment of our friendship. We couldn't take that chance.

We now had to find the balance. We quickly concluded that we had to turn to my parents right away and sell them on the idea of the project. The timing was right, because my father was just finishing up his exterior restoration contract of the Mont-Tremblant buildings. I knew that he had about $30,000 in liquidity at his disposal. I called my mother to mention that we had an investment project to propose, and that we had to meet to discuss it at greater length. She insisted on more information, but I clammed right up. We then set up a family dinner for the following Saturday at their lovely home in the Laurentians.

I had prepared a speech in my head to convince them that this was the opportunity of the century, a once-in-a-lifetime chance. Oddly, I sensed that the task would not be easy, and so I had additional arguments ready to respond to any doubts or questions that might arise at any time. Failure was not an option; we had to make, and win, our case. In a way, this would decide the life or death of our dream. And there was nothing better than visual aids to increase our chances of success. Therefore, we brought along a file containing all the questions and answers concerning the franchiser/franchisee, including the company history of the chain since its inception, the products it sold, etc...

That Saturday, the dinner was going very well. My mother had typically prepared a delicious meal. I made certain that my parents each had a little glass of wine in hand to make sure they were relaxed before we unveiled the project. After doing the dishes, my mother grew impatient for more information about our idea and asked if we were ready to sit down again to discuss the issue. At that point, I felt a little tension settle into my gut. I gathered up all my courage, knowing this was the moment of truth. Once we were seated at the table, I breathlessly rolled out my sales arguments non-stop. I even surprised myself. At the very end, once all my arguments were exhausted, I told them about the down payment required to secure the bank loan.

I proposed that they accommodate us with a loan of $25,000 over 2 years, and that we would pay them $5000 in interest at the end of the two-year period, as a return on their capital. They did not respond immediately, admitting that they felt it was car a major project that deserved some serious thought. My mother affirmed that she knew the restaurant chain well, as she had occasionally eaten lunch there with colleagues during her teaching career. My father followed up, adding that they had often visited one particular establishment in the chain as members of their pétanque (lawn bowling) league. That was one more ace up my sleeve. They already knew the chain well and were thrilled to rediscover it.

Much later in the evening, while out strolling alone with my father, he confessed that he was very interested in the project.

He even proceeded with his own proposition. He would provide the $25,000 as a partner in the business along with my mother, rather than simply granting is a loan. The idea of having my mother and father as partners had never crossed my mind. As I thought it, I realized it was the perfect formula. The more people who believed in the project, the better the chances that it would be a success. As the total down payment required was $100,000, their share of the profits was agreed upon at 25%. To simplify things, we decided by joint agreement that the deal would be set down in writing without delay. And today, after over 11 years, that deal remains valid. It was the best investment my parents had ever made in their lives. And for that matter, the best in ours.

And so, we were moving in the right direction. All that remained was to find a balance of $10,000. Chantal then came up with a great idea. She asked me to write her a letter confirming promise to hire, including future salary for her position in the business. She would use the letter to request a $5000 personal in her name from her bank. The request was approved, thanks to her sound credit rating. We just had to find the last $5000.

After having been turned down by various people, we had run out of ideas. That's when Chantal had a stroke of genius. She contacted her former boss, Daniel, with whom she had worked for a number of years. We presented him with the exact same proposal that we'd made to my parents. The deal we suggested meant that the loan would be reimbursed within one year, plus

$1000 as interest. He accepted, to our great relief. Daniel admitted that, although our presentation had been good, Chantal was the primary reason he had agreed. He explained that he had absolute faith in her. The loan was subsequently repaid as planned. And it's strange to see how events unfold, because two years later, he was the one asking us for a $15,000 loan to purchase a triplex. We agreed, with pleasure, in keeping with the principle of returning the favor. Everything went smoothly after that. He repaid us in accordance with our agreement and as a result of all this, our friendship reached a higher level because we had shared in a win-win situation. The issue of money was settled – on paper. However, there remained a significant next-to-last snag. I had to collect $15,000 by selling my house. The residence had been rented to a young couple for a year. And so, I suited up and headed off to pay them a visit. I made then a favorable offer, playing the franchise card and telling them that I was selling the house in order to start a business and make my dream come true. My proposition stated that they would have first option to purchase the property. I offered to include all the furnishings and appliances I owned. In addition, the seal-the-deal argument was that they did not have to lay down a penny of down payment. I would take care of that, and they would simply have to reimburse me in 18 months, without interest. In view of those favorable conditions, my asking price was non-negotiable. I was well aware that they loved the house, because before moving into my place, they had lived in a place one-quarter the size and poorly suited for their young family. After thinking about it for a week, they agreed. They wanted to purchase the house. Once again, the offer made everyone a winner. I'm happy for them today, because the value of the property has increased at least twofold since then.

The last but not least of the obstacles was finding the additional $25,000 in net working business capital. For readers wondering about that net working capital is, there's a simple answer: some bills must first be paid before the business opens, even before it has generated any sales. As an example: we had to pay $3000 as a security deposit to electric company. That amount was only returned to us 3 years later! Other similar bills and invoices also had to be paid before the business opened. After a few headaches in trying to find the $25,000, an idea occurred to me: I would head to the Business Development Bank of Canada, an organization that helps entrepreneurs with the start-up and expansion process. On my first visit to the branch, I was advised that before meeting with an agent, we had to fill out a 30-page business plan. No problem! The business plan was completed in two days. Several days later Chantal and I once again found ourselves obliged to make a sales pitch to secure this last crucial financing component. We gave it our all, with every ounce of passion and enthusiasm, knowing full well that this was the last step in the process.

Finally, after studying the dossier, the branch manager met with us and announced that our application had been approved. He asked us what we had said or done that was special during the first presentation to the agent responsible for the file. He was asking, he explained, because he had never seen a financing application for the restaurant business approved in the course of his 10-year career! We were very surprised to hear that, and it gave us a tremendous sense of pride. We were flattered. The interest rate was markedly higher than from a regular bank, given the risk incurred. However, we had no other option available. The loan term was set at 3 years. It was fully reimbursed in less than 6 months, saving us thousands of dollars in interest. So, do you think that everything comes easily to those who succeed? Think again, because I am sure we are not the only ones who've face this type of situation. We had to fight and pour an extraordinary amount of energy into making our dream a reality and, above all, to prevent it from slipping through our fingers. **Secret Number Twenty**: be persistent and find the capacity to avoid discouragement. The key point to retain from this chapter is that if you have decided to become financially independent, sooner or later you must take risks in starting a business, as we did. Be aware that the financing aspect is always complicated.

Don't wait until you have the entire sum required before making your first move, or you'll end up waiting until retirement age. When an opportunity presents itself, you will find the missing amount through perseverance, willpower and a good dose of ingenuity. Its incredible how much creativity can spring forth when you truly want something (with a passionate, burning desire). If you want to immerse yourself in the world of entrepreneurship for fun, I suggest you watch the TV program *Dragon's Den*. After a few episodes, you'll quickly discover that the financing aspect is the one sorely lacking for most entrepreneurs. In my experience, I can tell you that it is a thousand times easier to secure financing for a home or a vehicle than it is for a business. Also, prepare a solid dossier before approaching a bank. In the TV program, you'll also note that any candidate who shows up without a sound, concrete plan behind their project will be rebuffed by the Dragons. Rest assured that bankers are not very different from the Dragons. They do not like risk and uncertainty. You have to demonstrate and prove that they will recover their stake within the specified timeframe.

TRAINING

"Learn the fundamentals of the game and stick to them. Band-aid remedies never last."

Jack Nicklaus

Professional golfer

Do you constantly, instinctively seek to improve yourself in unfamiliar areas, or domains you have not yet mastered? Successful people tend to constantly feed their desire for new knowledge. Today, with Internet tools like Youtube and Google, increasing or deepening your understanding in a bottomless range of subjects has never been so easy and accessible. The info is abundant, and it's all free. All you have to do is dig into the research and you can find any information you want in every conceivable subject. I also strongly advise you to attend seminars on the subjects that most strongly interest you. Invest in your future and set aside an annual amount, let's say $750, exclusively reserved for self-improvement. Do not forget that, as a general rule, we apply only 10% of what we learn from books. And that is why I read constantly. Every time I finish a book, the next one is waiting on the bedside table. Over the years, 10% of that makes a considerable difference. Seminars and training sessions are much more effective, but also more expensive. Therefore, make sure that they're genuinely worthwhile to you.   They say that good training is worth its weight in gold. Chantal and I were very eager to quit our respective jobs and embark on this great adventure as soon as possible. Chantal had no trouble leaving her job. Her last words to her saddened colleagues were: "So long everyone, I know I'm headed for better things!" My experience was similar. I was truly happy at the idea of becoming a businessman at the age of 25. **Secret Number Twenty-One**: you must leave your comfort zone if you want to pull yourself up to a higher level.

Our training began on December 12, 2000. We were booked into a condensed training schedule because our opening date was swiftly approaching. And by "condensed training," I mean 16 hours on some days, 7 days a week without a break. We suddenly lost all sense of the passage of days of the week and hours in the day. I'd thought the training would practically be a vacation... It was quite a shock. I can tell you that it resembled a military camp much more than a holiday. However, it was high-quality training, and it reflected the reality of operating a restaurant open 24 hours a day, 7 days a week. We also realized that working as an employee bore no resemblance to working as an entrepreneur. They were two completely different planets, the latter involving problems to be solved every hour of the day, even on Christmas and New Year's Day, because the business never closes!

For your reading pleasure, there are the tasks we devoted every hour of the day to: making pastries and baked goods from A to Z as though we'd made them at home (yes, you read that right). Making cake icing. Cleaning every corner of the kitchen with a toothbrush. Starting over, starting over, and starting over again. And when something wasn't perfect: redo, redo, and yes, redo again. It was brainwashing, but at the same time, it was a test to see if we were going to weather the storm. It was all normal. But when you're immersed in that soup, you feel as though you're going completely mad. Above all, 16 hours of standing on a ceramic floor making pastries, 7 days of the week, is not the best way to keep your legs in good shape. Chantal and I were convinced that our legs were throbbing with so much pain that they were going to explode. In the little time we were afforded for sleep, they ached so badly that we could barely sleep. Chantal then had the bright idea of heading to the pharmacy to find a jar of Deep Cold ointment to soothe our aching muscles. Unfortunately, it didn't really work. We kept our training schedule handy, and at the end of every day, gleefully drew a big black X through it on the calendar. That's how we kept our spirits up. A Vancouver couple was in training at the same time we were. They were friendly and we stood together through the adventure. However, things did not work out as well for them. His wife missed 70% of the training. Her husband explained that she was homesick. We also felt very alone and far from home. Albert Einstein stated that time is relative, and a week can seem like an eternity or a millisecond, depending on your level of pleasure or pain. As someone who has put the theory to the test, I can confirm he was correct.

We stayed in the neighboring municipality of Burlington in the basement of lovely prosperous-looking home. We accessed our room via a side door. It was large and well-suited for us. The owner was a lovely woman. She explained that we were the umpteenth clients of the chain to stay in her home. She had been referred to us by the parent company before we had set out, since this option was more affordable than staying in the hotel we had chosen. Also, we could cook our own meals. The budgetary aspect was extremely critical at the time, as our salaries were basically nonexistent. Our budget only allowed us to spend $90 per week on food. We ate a ton of potatoes cooked 1,001 ways during those 2 months. However, food was free when we were at the head office, which helped us a lot.

Christmas day was swiftly approaching, and we were nervously wondering whether we would be spending the holiday in Ontario or at home. We ended up having a choice: Christmas Day or New Year's Day. Christmas was our first choice, and to our great surprise, we were afforded 4 days off, December 23-26. Suddenly, hope sprung anew in our hearts. The last few remaining days of work became relatively easy and enjoyable.

Strangely, since the beginning of training, it had snowed almost non-stop every day, always falling softly and gently. Nonetheless, it caused traffic jams day and night. On December 23, happily, it was time to head home. Once again, it snowed – but this time, heavily. Regardless, we took to the road, making sure to drive as carefully as possible. Staying away from our loved ones for any longer was unthinkable. During the trip, though, we saw at least 25 trucks swallowed up by snowbanks, prompting the realization that we'd made a risky decision. By the grace of God we arrived at our destination intact, despite an additional 2 hours of slogging through the snow. Needless to say, our family found we were pale and tired that holiday. That little vacation did us a world of good. The only problem was that, on December 26, our brains fired off messages to our respective selves stating that they had no desire whatsoever to return and finish the training. Fortunately, reason prevailed.

In all, the training was no barrel of monkeys, but we are proud to have gotten through it. **Secret Number Twenty-Two**: being prepared to experience difficult moments in the short term to reap much greater rewards in the long term is a strategy that leads straight to success. We were able to focus our minds on the ultimate goal: the official opening of our business on February 4, 2001

RUNNING A BUSINESS

"Nobody can change the past, but we can

all determine our future."

Colin Powell

U.S. Secretary of State

Are you paralyzed by the fear of failure? In fact, fear is an integral part of every human being and one must be bold to master it. To this day, whenever a new investment rears its head, I personally feel a twinge of fear. As time has passed, I have realized it is impossible to completely eliminate it because, at the basic level, fear exists to protect us. **Secret Number Twenty-Three**: knowing how to master your fears is crucial for anyone who wants to succeed. The more deeply you analyze and research your potential investments, the more fear will come to replace faith. The goal is to become aware of the role fear plays in your life and to prevent it from playing to big a role in your decisions. One good method is to address it directly and say: "Thank you for the role that you play, you are truly useful, but if you don't mind, please don't uselessly prevent me from going forward, because I want to fully realize my potential." You will see your fear melt away like snow in the sunshine.

Don't forget that it's always possible to hit a home run, the kind of masterstroke that can send you soaring to financial victory. Here, I must make an important aside. As you know, homers are much less common in baseball than singles or doubles. Should you therefore concentrate on home runs and forget about the other hits? Absolutely not – and that's the mistake made by the majority of people. They look for the quick homer that will make them rich overnight and pass on the singles, the doubles and even the triples! One of the secrets of wealthy people is that they do exactly the opposite. They achieve many small and medium-sized victories and bet on a high volume of transactions to build their fortunes. Sometimes they hit a home run, but that isn't the primary goal, because they know that it's the number of transactions all put together that matters most. If you wait for the perfect home run, you run the risk of waiting there your whole life, without hitting a single one.

As you can see, the Mont-Tremblant investment was just a single for us, since we only made a few thousand dollars in profit from the sale of the unit. It certainly didn't make us rich. However, that single allowed us to hit a double with the contract for the exterior renovation of the buildings. The rest of the story is a home run that was made possible thanks to a single and a double. My spouse and I hit our big home run on Sunday, February 4, 2001. However, we didn't have the slightest idea of that at the time. The long-awaited opening day finally arrived, and it was very emotional. I remember waking that morning of February 4, 2001 with the gentle sense of having finally reached the ultimate goal. In my mind, the assault course segment was ending and a new life was looming before us. However, reality would soon catch up to us. As you will see, a new life was certainly awaiting us, but the assault course had only begun. A few minutes after waking, Chantal and I headed gently towards our brand-spanking-new restaurant. We were proud, and extremely eager to experience the long-awaited moment, like a new mother about to give birth. As we arrived, my parents were in the restaurant, accompanied by our new employees nervously awaiting the fateful moment. Many employees from the parent company were also on hand to show their support and sort out the final details.

The official photo was taken around 10 a.m. As soon as it was done, the official opening signal was given. My district manager, the person designated by the parent company, handed me the key to the front door, saying: "Dany will unlock the door, and then you can throw away the key if you'd like, because you won't need it anymore!" (The business would remain open 24 hours a day / 365 days a year). A few seconds after the grand opening, the first customer crossed the threshold. Our dream had come true: we were officially in business. I will always remember the look on the customer's face as he entered, completely surprised to learn that he was the very first to enter our restaurant. We kept and framed that first $5 bill as a souvenir but, even more so, to bring us luck, because we needed it. We hoped that they would "reproduce" endlessly, that it would be a good omen of prosperity to come. During that day, customer patronage was moderate to low, which, of course was in no way abnormal. A good few members of our family showed up, out of curiosity and also to encourage us. At the end of the day, our assessment was clear: the restaurant was new, and we had to create customer habits and build up customer loyalty. We had a lot of work ahead of us in order to increase turnover and reach the point of profitability. With an average bill of several dollars per customer, we would have to serve zillions of them to cover our operating expenses.

The following days resembled opening day – which is to say, with very modest results. The first week ended with $11,000 in sales. I knew we would lose money with sales volume that low, a very stressful, unpleasant feeling that makes you feel permanently queasy. The second week was a little better, with $13,000 – but still written in red ink. Fortunately, growth continued apace. After a month and a half of operations, we had reached $17,000, and could therefore pay our employees' salaries and most of our current invoices (ouch!). It was only a matter of time before we took flight.

During the first two weeks following our opening, we were lucky to be ably to rely on a special team provided by the parent company to help us train our 20 newly-hired employees. The day that training team left us was a little like a mother bird pushing her fledglings out of the nest. Chantal and I were not fully prepared to take on a level of stress and commitments that high. I remember watching as Chantal burst into tears that first day because of the intense pressures of business operations and various problems. Those are the moments when doubt creeps in and you ask yourself the question: "what have I gotten myself into here... have I really done the right thing?" in addition to dealing with loss-making turnover, we experienced a lot of problems with our employees. Some of them had quit. They didn't like the work, and Chantal or I had fired some others for all sorts of reasons (incompetence, theft, attitude problems with other employees etc...). As an immediate consequence, we found ourselves with a chronic shortage of employees during all work shifts. Ultimately, triple our efforts and work 100-hour weeks on average during that first year! There were even several occasions when we worked 24 hours without even being able to sleep. Getting late-night phone calls at home was commonplace. Employment applications were scarce and the quality of candidates was low. That did not help our cause, merely adding stress, because our revenue was climbing non-stop. Admittedly, that was a good problem to have. Our experience could have been summarized as: a series of contradictory situations, from the highs to the lows...The thing that allowed us to endure it all was the fact that we were a couple, and that in difficult moments when one of us was tempted to give it all up (and sometimes that temptation was very strong), the other would intervene, saying: "I didn't come this far and make all this effort just to throw in the towel." Also, watching our turnover climb, we knew we were betting on the winning horse.

Chantal and I had determined our respective fields of activity in advance, which is my **Secret Number Twenty-Four**: always plan out who will be doing what before you venture into whatever business you choose. That will avoid plenty of potential conflicts. I handled suppliers, orders, and everything that involved administration. Chantal handled hiring, operational standards, pay and everything that involved human resources. In broad terms, that remains the way we operate. Each of us knows what he/she has to do and does not interfere in the other's jurisdiction.

The final factor that played in our favor concerned my parents. They were of enormous help to us in those first two years. My father had decided to give up the construction business to take charge of the dining room of the restaurant and dishwashing. In addition to taking care of those tasks, he spent a lot of time speaking with customers, who ended up thinking *he* was the franchisee. That connection with our clientele helped build customer loyalty and increase patronage as the months passed. My mother handled personnel management in concert with Chantal. Whenever we took a day off, my parents were there to look after our common interests, and vice versa. Without them, we probably wouldn't have survived or, at the very least, would have ended up even more exhausted. I don't even know if that is humanly possible. We stuck together as a family, and that was undoubtedly one of our greatest strengths.

In our first year, during the provincial convention, we collected our first award: among all the restaurants that had opened that year, we were the champions in total sales volume. We were thrilled to be recognized as such, and certainly felt it had been earned. Year Number Two featured phenomenal growth, with sales rising +60% compared to the first year. We truly had an extraordinary franchise on our hands. Our business had suddenly been transformed into a moneymaking machine. However, we still had problems recruiting employees. As a result, we had a lot of trouble keeping pace with our sales growth. Fortunately, year number two witnessed an improvement in the number of hours worked – the light at the end of the tunnel! We were now working an average of 50 hours a week. We had managed to find an employee in our team with the skills required to take on a managerial position. He proved to be a good choice, because he knew how to take care of his responsibilities. This was of great help to us over the five years that followed. The reason we had to work so hard during those first years was that the restaurant was constantly overflowing with customers, inside as well as outside, in the drive-through service, 7 days a week (even at Christmastime). It had therefore become necessary for us to be on the floor with our employees almost all the time to properly manage the customer traffic. It wasn't rare to see the line of customers stretching right out of the restaurant! Little by little, we realized that if we could become more efficient in our drive-through service time, it would increase sales prodigiously, not to mention shortening the lines inside the restaurant. We've never stopped growing since then, with increased sales year after year. The winning elements were there, and the business loan had been completely reimbursed within 18 months. It was unprecedented in the history of the chain.

After three successful years, we were finally ready to take on another challenge and make the big leap into opening a second restaurant. We followed exactly the same procedure as we had at the beginning. We notified the parent company that we were interested in acquiring a second establishment. They provided us with the steps and criteria to follow in order to qualify. In short: be an operational leader in all aspects of the business and follow standards to the letter. We worked very hard to generate the necessary results, and the following year, a second opportunity came about. Once again, it was a new restaurant located about 7 kilometers away from the other. The second restaurant was very well located along side a highway. Like its "big brother", the first weeks were very slow, which is to say, in the red (heavy financial losses). With all of our experience, we knew the recipe to boost sales: patience, work, execution. And that's precisely what we did. To speed up the process, I made a proposal to my spouse. It was then February, and weekly sales were $12,000. I gave her a challenge: if she could increase weekly sales to $18,000 between then and June, she would win an all-expenses-paid trip to Spain as her reward.

I probably don't need to tell you that she poured all the effort necessary into the task and won the prize, even meeting the challenge a few weeks before the month of June. The three-week trip was very expensive, but also ranked as one of the best of our lives. The second restaurant has been growing ever since, year after year, with a growth curve similar to the first. With time and patience, we found we'd hit a second home run.

Building a prosperous business is no vacation, as you can see. If you appreciate the peace of mind that comes with a Mondayto-Friday job, having a business would make you unhappy. The beauty of being employed rests in the fact that when problems arise, your superior or your boss handles them. And when the weekend arrives, you can relax without a care in the world. You don't always have that luxury when you are an entrepreneur. Here is a good example. Recently, my telephone rang one fine Sunday afternoon. It was our manager. He explained that there was a serious problem at the restaurant. A client who using the drive-through service had carelessly tossed his cigarette butt on the ground. It had rolled into a tiny fissure between the asphalt and our exterior wall. A few seconds later, fire spread to the interior of the wall and the fire department had to be called in. fortunately, no one was hurt, and the damages were minor. However, the restaurant had to be closed temporarily for over three hours. As a matter of routine procedure, the firemen had to contact the Ministère de l'Agriculture, des Pêcheries et de l'Alimentation (the ministry that governs restaurants) to inform them of the situation, since smoke had seeped into the inside of the restaurant. An employee of the ministry then telephoned us with a list of what we had to do before being allowed to reopen the restaurant.

All in all, the incident cost us approximately $3000 in losses. It's incredible how problematic a seemingly innocuous incident can become! And we've got a file full of dozens of similarly unlikely tales. So, you can clearly see that all of this is no walk in the park, right? You must tell yourself that having a business is a little like having a child and that you are definitely in the parent role in the adventure. Having employees is also similar to having children. You must treat them in a fair and equal manner if you want to maintain harmony among the troops, and remain aware that without them, you could not possibly operate. They are at the very heart of the enterprise. Having the qualities of a psychologist and good listening skills are also essential assets, because your employees are certain to tell you about the problems that afflict them in their daily lives. Today, with over 100 employees in our business, our little family has become   fairly   large   indeed.

THE SKY'S THE LIMIT

"You never get past a barrier,

you only push it further in front of you."

Robert Sabatier

Author

There are many ways to manage a business, and the results will vary widely depending on the management style you adopt. My own personal management style has evolved considerably over the years. The first style that seemed appropriate at the time was the "One Man Show." I wanted to do everything myself because I was convinced that I was the only one capable of doing things properly. I made sure to stick my nose into everything and loved to swagger around. With time, I discovered that wanting to do it all on your own will soon make you irritable, with the exhaustion of daily stress lying in wait around every corner. When the One Man Show is on, problems are few and things go smoothly. However, this is not the best method. When you are away from the business, on vacation for example, nothing works anymore and everything comes crashing down like a house of cards. When the cat's away, the mice will play. I must mention, though, that at the very outset of a business, you will probably have to use this style, because you may not have the budget to pay for a management team. The idea is to adapt your style along the way as your business grows and evolves.

I have also witnessed a management style that was never my own, which we call the "laisser faire" style. This one is the most disastrous style that I know. Indeed, those who adopt this mode of operation are incompetents of the first order, afflicted with a host of problems. Here's a list of the common symptoms: customers systematically desert the establishment, internal theft runs rampant, customer service is generally pathetic, employees are unmotivated, bad hygiene and cleanliness habits are commonplace, etc… it's usually only a matter of time, but this group always ends in failure.

Next comes the pyramid style, which is **Secret Number Twenty-Five**. This has been my style for a number of years, and it works perfectly. The pyramid has four levels. Starting with the highest, there is the president, followed by the second level, the management team. In our business, the management team comprises a manager and an assistant-manager per establishment. The third level consists of supervisors and trainers in the various work shifts. The fourth level consists of the members of the team. The responsible parties at every level are charged with looking after the level below and with following the directives from the level above. My role, at the highest level, is to properly and effectively communicate all the goals that must be reached to the second level, the manager and the assistant-manager. The objective is to reward good behavior as often as possible. Therefore, when goals are reached, a performance bonus is awarded to the second level in each quarter (three months) according to the goals attained. These cover all controllable and critical aspects of the business. **Secret Number Twenty-Six**: Never micro-manage. When you are in the highest level (level one), you must never, ever micro-manage (that is, interfere in) levels three and four, because that is tantamount to doing the work allocated to level two.

At level two, the managers in turn set their own objectives to be achieved by the supervisors and trainers. Finally, there are rewards for good behavior for the fourth level, the members of the team, for performance and results. All aspects of accounting are handled by an external auditor who specializes in our field, and I suggest you do the same. Let each person have his or her area of expertise. Every month, we receive an accounting report on costs. Using that report, we can verify if the management team has reached the goals set for them. When the two cornerstones of level two attain a success rate of 80% and over for all goals set, it indicates that they are working very well with the rest of the team. Those rates are set high, but can be attained with a constant focus. If your management team consistently reaches 70% or less of the objectives set for them, those figures reveal that they are not cut out for the work and must be replaced by more competent people. The higher the bonus awarded to the management team, the higher the performance level of business at every level. And performance means profitability. Also, when the time comes to hire a manager or an assistant, you must ensure that he is more competent than you for the job he will be performing. Yes, you read that correctly. I personally make use of headhunters in this domain. They are very expensive, but in my business, it is crucial to have a management team qualified to deliver extraordinary results. And believe me, the formula works. As I write these lines, I am in my home office, where I've hung at least 10 operational excellence awards received since we opened. I cannot fail to mention how much we love to encourage good performance. However, we also act promptly in dealing with misbehavior or performance that harms the team.

From the moment of hiring, we set the bar very high, and future members of the team are made aware of our high expectations. The final point here, which is **Secret Number Twenty-Seven**, is that you must like your employees. Those who are incompetent, whom you hate for that very fact alone, must absolutely be fired without delay. Automatically, those who remain and make up your core will be the people who achieve your standards of quality. Then, all that remains is to fall in love with your team! When people feel appreciated, they tend to pay you back one hundredfold in terms of productivity. I honestly have a boundless adoration for my employees, and I believe they appreciate me in return. In-house, even though we operate a pyramid management style, we can feel a bond that unites us, which greatly resembles a family bond. We are like a small close-knit family, and we work together for the good of the group. When you achieve this balance in the enterprise, the sky's the limit.

TRIAL AND ERROR

"Sometimes by losing a battle, you find a new way to win the war."

Donald Trump

Real estate billionaire

Have you ever dreamed of being your own boss and freeing yourself from the routine of your current work environment? If you answered *yes*, congratulations! I encourage you to continue along that path and become the creator of your own destiny. The question that immediately follows is: what is keeping you from acting on it right now? Of course, you are not obligated to quit your job this very minute. The goal is to keep your job as long as possible, the way my spouse and I did. We quit our respective jobs at the right moment, because we had an opportunity in hand that provided us with a way forward. I advise you to take action in the same way. Out of necessity, if your project is a failure, you will at least have the personal satisfaction of having tried everything you could. That way, you can live the rest of your life with a clear conscience. You do not want to find yourself at age 70 sitting in a rocking chair, saying to yourself: "I should have given it a shot!" **Secret**

Number Twenty-Eight: pursue your ideas all the way. I personally experienced this 5 years back. At that time, success stuck to me like glue, and I had the false impression that everything I touched turned to gold. I came up with the idea of investing in the field of nanotechnology. After several hours of research on the Internet, I was amazed to discover that there were no specialty funds in this promising sector. A stroke of genius crossed my mind: I would start up my own specialty fund in nanotechnology. Since I was the first person to step establish such a fund, I expected immediate success. Calling a renowned law firm, I requested they prepare a document describing the legal steps required to set up my brilliant project. A short time later, I'd found the name and logo of the company. However, the legal document proved to be a disappointment. What had seemed a simple idea at first was far from it, because the mutual fund industry required a mountain of paperwork.

In all, launching the fund required a bare minimum of $250,000 in legal fees of all sorts, just to be in accordance with the government agencies that monitor this business sector. I was facing a wrenching decision: pursue my idea all the way and risk never having it launch, or simply drop it. At this point, you must understand that my project was already quite advanced: the company had been formed, I had in the meantime finished the courses required to obtain a license to practice, the logo, fund prospectus and website were also set up, and finally, there were the legal fees to create the legal opinion. In short, the fees had already added up to several thousand dollars, but much more spending was required to make the idea a reality. Then, several days after acquiring the license to practice, my lawyer informed me that I shouldn't forget that one of the numerous prerequisites for managing an investment fund was having several years of prior experience. I told him to absolutely stop everything as quickly as possible. The project was dead and buried that very day. In all, a sum of $15,000 was swallowed up by that adventure. On the positive side, however, I had the satisfaction of at least having tried. I am consoled by the knowledge that it all could have been worse. The major error I advise you to avoid, and which would have allowed me to reduce my losses, is following the steps in the wrong order. In my specific case, by being more patient and waiting for the legal opinion, it would have been possible to see that the idea was not viable for a person in my situation. As you can see, setting a good idea in motion is not without risk. **Secret Number Twenty-Nine**: sometimes you have to set your ego aside, accept defeat and move on to something else. It's all part of the "game."

The most important thing is to win more often than you lose. You've probably noticed that not even the best hockey player in the world scores on every shot. Rest assured that the principle is always the same in business.

THE VAUNTED LAW OF ATTRACTION

"You create your own universe

as you go along."

Winston Churchill

Prime Minister of Great Britain

Have you ever asked yourself why some people are always lucky, while others seem to have been born under a bad sign? It is an interesting question.

Using real-life examples, this chapter aims to explain les the broad outlines of the law of attraction, but above all, to demonstrate how it works. If you want a deeper understanding of the law as such, there are plenty of books on the subject. For instance, have you read Rhonda Byrne's bestseller, *The Secret*? If you answered no, I suggest that you read it, because it is a sound piece of writing overall. In a nutshell, the reader learns a universal principle that has been used throughout history and which is exceedingly simple: you attract what your thoughts express, day after day, whether they are good or bad for you.

Thoughts emit frequencies (a little like cellphone frequencies) that are picked up by the universe (or the Divinity, if you prefer) and interpreted as an order, without making distinctions between them. The universe sends us what we have asked it for, time after time. Surely you will have understood that it is therefore important to know how to coordinate your thoughts in a positive direction to receive all that you truly desire. Above all, you must avoid negative thoughts and emotions, because that will be what you attract in your daily life. Does all of this seem a little too simplistic? It is not.

Moreover, I think that is the reason the book was so hugely successful. We North Americans are the world champions at wanting to do the least possible and have it all without making too much of an effort. We are all fond of this type of theory, because it requires very little aside from aligning our thoughts in the right, positive direction. Which is not always clearly evident, incidentally. If you adhere to the principle of the book to the letter, it amounts to saying that anyone who settles comfortably into a chair for the entire day and thinks in a positive manner will receive as much money as he desires, and that it will all happen by magic! I'm sorry to burst your bubble, but that is not exactly how it happens.

However, that does not mean that I reject the entire contents of the book – far from it. It contains plenty of truths. In order to embrace the theory, you must understand and accept that everything that has happened in your life up to the present moment is the result of what you have personally drawn to yourself. It's hard to believe, isn't it? That's right! Everything is your fault, and nobody else's. Sorry, there's no room for excuses. Over time, I have discovered that people have a pronounced tendency to believe that their destiny is preordained and that they have no influence over events. Personally, I do not believe in destiny. Rather, I believe that it is a theory invented for people who want a sense of meaning in their lives. No. I would much rather believe that our page is blank when we are born and that we can write whatever and as much as we wish upon it. We all have free will.

These are my personal beliefs on the subject of the Law of Attraction. All I know is that it works, and that's good enough for me. If you ask me why a ball or any other object you drop falls inexorably towards the ground, I will tell you that it is due to the Law of Gravity. It is impossible to escape or alter that reality. The principle is the same for the Law of Attraction. To deny or refuse to believe in it does not change the fact that it is present and in action at all times. I have witnessed so many circumstances in my life that support the theory that it is impossible for me to ignore it.

My parents offer the best example. In their town, they are the undisputed masters when it comes to the beauty of their landscaping. Their flowers take center stage, and it isn't rare to see passersby stop to snap a few photos of the scene. Indeed, they've won first prize every year they've entered the annual municipal beautification contest. Lately, they've even given up participating because they want someone else to have a chance!

Step number 1: have a clear desire. Every year, my parents have a desire, to have a piece of land where life is good and lush flowers bloom. Step number 2: act in harmony with this desire. They plant their tiny seeds one by one at the beginning of the season, already able to imagine the final result. Step number 3: Let Go, but without losing sight of the ultimate goal. The Infinite Intelligence will take care of the miracles to come. From that point, my parents' labors are relatively minimal: they water the seeds when rain is sparse and weed from time to time. They keep the faith and never doubt in the process, even though, in the beginning, there is no result visible to the naked eye. As a passing spectator every year, I can tell you that their final results have always been spectacular. My question to you is: do you truly believe they would produce the same results simply by imagining a piece of land filled with beautiful flowers while excluding the other steps? Nonetheless, one mustn't be naïve about this either.

Now you understand how this law works. **Secret Number Thirty**: use the Law of Attraction as stipulated above for all that you desire and you will witness miracles occurring in your life. There is, however, a very important caveat. If, in setting your goal, you have a dominant feeling of doubt within yourself, then you must redefine your desire. Without deep conviction, a sincerity of feeling, there is no chance of your desire coming true. Doubt is your mortal enemy. You must, in a sense, feel in harmony with your desire, as though it were a reality that is inevitably on its way towards you. Once I discovered this theory, I was delighted. I decided to put it to the test in my daily life without further delay. Acquiring my franchises is probably the best example. I felt a powerful desire to become an entrepreneur. I took steps to ensure that I was in harmony with my desire and the universe responded favorably to it. If I had not followed the right process and responded to the franchisers' requests, the universe would have been completely powerless to address my desire. "God helps those that help themselves" is a phrase that perfectly applies to this Law.

One day, I decided to set the bar exceedingly high and test the law to the limit. This was in 2005. Chantal and I had our two restaurants. The first generated a turnover of 2 million dollars per year and the second restaurant brought in 1 million dollars. I therefore expressed my desire to push sales to 3 million and 2 million respectively for each restaurant, and to do so within two years. I wrote the two goals down prominently in my Life Project notebook. Growing overall sales in two establishments by 2 millions dollars in so little time was no mean feat. It involved increasing restaurant patronage by 700,000 customers per year! And so I resolutely decided to put the Law into action.

You probably want to know what the results of this experiment were, don't you? Two years later, we ended the process with 2.95 million in sales at the first restaurant and 1.9 million at the second. We had met the target, and we far surpassed it the following year. Do you think I burst in to tears believing the law didn't work simply because the original objectives had not been fully met? Not at all. On the contrary, I was totally pumped, and ever since, I've lost any fear of setting goals that seem impossible at the outset.

Since the Law of Attraction works for everyone and works all the time, I believe that in the preceding case, the goals weren't fully reached because a sense of doubt had probably settled into my mind along the way. That prevented me from reaching 100% of the objectives. I caused this, the Law did not. It is not always easy to use the Law of Attraction the way we should, because that little interior negative voice sometimes intrudes to sabotage the process.

Try to think of the Law of Attraction as a game of darts. When you aim at the center of the board with absolute concentration, you have an excellent chance of hitting the bulls-eye or at least coming close to it. Now try that exercise with your eyes closed (in other words: like someone who does not know about the Law, or doesn't use it to his advantage). And good luck with the wall around that dartboard! Are you still unconvinced that this vaunted law exists? The following story will probably convince you a little more. It concerns my manager, Steve. One day, I gave him *The Secret* as a gift, telling him he might find it very useful. A few days later, he professed his delight in knowing about the Law and mentioned that the timing was apt, as he had always wanted a Tag watch. It was therefore his turn to put the Law to the test. I was curious to find out what would happen, and encouraged him in the process. That evening during dinner at home, he shared the story with his wife, Carole, describing the model and color of the watch he wanted. Of course, Carole had not read the book, and scoffed at the entire notion. Several weeks passed without anything particularly eventful happening. Then, one fine day when I was on vacation with the family in Orlando, Steve called me, in a bit of a panic. (He never calls me when I am on vacation). He told me that a customer had come into the restaurant the evening before, with a leather fanny pack that strapped around his waist. Unfortunately, the fanny pack became detached while he was sitting and eating, and slid under the table. The customer left the restaurant without realizing it. I should probably mention that this infamous pack contained $25,000 in cash!

A few minutes later, someone in the restaurant found the fanny pack in question. He went out into the parking lot and turned the bag in to one of our employees a few minutes later, stating that he had found it outside (and of course, it was empty). As you can well imagine, the owner of the fanny pack returned to the restaurant several hours later. The problem was that he accused our employee of having found the fanny pack in the dining room and having kept the money. The heat, as they say, was on.

The following day, Steve checked our cameras for a clearer picture of the story. Fortunately, our restaurant is equipped with

18 digital color cameras located in every section. Contacting the customer once again, Steve told him the entire story, mentioning that our employee was not guilty and that we had video proof of same. Needless to say, the customer wanted to see the videos; moreover, he requested a copy of the tape, telling Steve that he would offer us a gift if we agreed to his request – which was why Steve had called me in Orlando. He wanted my approval before going forward, and also wanted to share the unusual story with me. Without a moment's hesitation, I gave him the green light to make the video copies. However, I mentioned to Steve that no gift was expected in return. The following morning, Steve contacted me again, even more nervous now because he was actually with the customer, who wanted the copies we'd promised but also insisted that we accept his gift. And so I simply told Steve: I won't accept a gift, but you can if you're too nervous to have to turn him down. He confessed that he was feeling the heat and wanted to be done with the story as quickly as possible.

One hour later, Steve called me a final time, sounding relieved. He had accepted the gift and handed over the video copies to the customer, who seemed very happy and satisfied with how we had cooperated with him. The gift Steve received was... a Tag watch in the exact model and color he had visualized several weeks earlier!!! Furthermore, it was no counterfeit, as it had been delivered in the original box with the instructions. The moral of this story: never underestimate the Law of Attraction. It is powerful, and it can bring you everything you desire. However, the thing you desire may arrive in an unorthodox manner, as was the case with Steve. This story is a marvelous demonstration of how the Law operates, but I still sense a trace of skepticism in your mind. No problem: I have a second recent anecdote to offer. Every year for the past 3, my parents have vacationed in Florida. At first, they stayed for three months. They had so thoroughly enjoyed their experience that, the following year, they extended their stay for four months. Last year, it was five months and yes, you've guessed it, this year they'll spend six months in all. During my last visit to their condo in Florida this past Christmas, my father made a shocking revelation. Because they had always rented their unit up to that point, a 6-month lease would amount to them having to spend $9000 for the 2012-2013 season. When my father mentioned the amount, my blood pressure shot right up. I had spent a year searching for a condo for them in my spare time. However, this was also the moment when I recognized the urgency of the situation. I suggested to the family that we collectively purchase a family property rather than a condo, because then we could all use it. My brother, his wife, my parents and Chantal were very excited by this idea. In our agreement, my parents would invest that money in the family home rather than pour it into a lease. We decided to leap into intensive search mode towards July in order to notarize the property deed around the month of September. My parents were due to be in Florida by parents October 15.

As anticipated, by June, I figured the time was now or never to get serious about the project. I had decided to put the Law of Attraction to work. The family consensus was: we were looking for a house with at least 4 bedrooms, 3 bathrooms and a living area of at least 3000 square feet with a double garage, built sometime between 2000 and 2007. Our list was very specific, and wanted to be in the West Palm Beach area. My parents also had one condition, that they did not want a house that needed renovations. Our price would have to land between $250,000 and $300,000 (when you shop for property in the U.S., you have to pay in cash, because there is no financing available to Canadians). I also added my own criteria to the list. I wanted the house to have clay tile roofing and beige exterior walls, in the Tuscan style. To bring the Law of Attraction into further action, I found and cut out a picture of a house in a magazine that matched the one we wanted in every respect. I framed the picture and hung it on a wall in my office, in full view of my desk so that I could see it whenever I was using my computer. Our first weeks of househunting were unsuccessful and frustrating. Whenever I thought I'd found a gem, someone in the family would find fault with it. When there were no faults with the house itself, the location was problematic (the wrong coast of Florida, or in a remote area). In short, I was a little discouraged. That's when I decided to Let Go, as the formula recommends. The decision bore fruit, because a few days later, our real estate agent had conducted an intensive search on our behalf and sent us twenty potential properties. Strangely, only one truly captured our attention, and for good reason: it was the house that perfectly suited our criteria. The entire family was delighted, and agreed. That was when Chantal made the following confession to us: "It's strange, but I feel that this is the right one and that this time, it'll be ours." That very day, we sent the purchase offer to the seller and, after a counter-proposal, the offer was accepted without a hitch. The inspection of the property was excellent, the house was impeccable and as a bonus, all the appliances were brand new. The only thing that didn't exactly match our list was the living area, which was perfect, since the property was slightly larger than we'd sought: 3200 square feet. We picked up the property for half the selling price it had gone for as a new house in 2003. And best of all, it's located in West Palm Beach!

Have I succeeded in convincing all the skeptics? You have to be realistic: you will always find people who will discourage you in your projects. That is why I advise you to use the Law of Attraction yourself, or to share your experiences exclusively with positive people whom you trust implicitly. I call them dream-breakers or dream-stealers, and they are everywhere. Beware, and avoid them like the plague. Some people have even told me that such and such a thing would have happened in my life anyway, with or without the Law of Attraction. Whenever I hear that kind of comment, I avoid confiding in those people again.

The only thing that's truly important to me is that the Law of Attraction works. And by the way, it was Steve who taught me **Secret Number Thirty-One**: when something works, never change it. I learned that lesson when I spotted a new instant drink machine in our purchase catalogues. Steve remarked that our current machine worked just fine, and dropped that famous phrase mentioned above. I ignored him, and it cost us dearly. The new machine was complicated and often out of order. The lost sales piled up, and after two years, I finally resigned myself to the fact that I had to throw the $17,000 machine in the garbage. And what did Steve say? I told you so! Since then, I have never repeated the mistake. (Thanks, Steve). Not using the Law of Attraction can also prove to be a costly error in your life, depriving you of all the wonderful projects that you might have accomplished. As I read up on the Law of Attraction, I naturally became interested in quantum physics. Be careful here, because this is science and not some idle theory. Quantum physics teaches us and proves that we are all interconnected. There is no separation between you and me or anyone else, and we are all one. Time is an illusion of the mind and does not exist. The reality that we know exists solely in our imagination. We are all one and the same consciousness. It also teaches us that we find ourselves in many places simultaneously in other dimensions (incredible, isn't it)? You can find a very good BBC report on this on Youtube, in which internationally renowned scientists inform us that there are may be 12 different simultaneous dimensions! If we push the idea a little further, it amounts to saying that whenever you have a thought, it instantly becomes a reality in another dimension. The idea becomes exciting, doesn't it? Personally, I'm very eager to hear the answers that science will bring us in the years to come part. And there will be answers. Just look at the world's largest laboratory and research center, built for 6 billion dollars in Switzerland (the CERN). It is a center specializing in particle physics. In their laboratories, the scientists at CERN recreate the conditions that existed just after the Big Bang and study the evolution of matter since the birth of the universe. Twenty different countries are participating in this adventure, which employs 2400 physicists (in fact, one out of every two physicists in the world is from the CERN).

I know that all of this seems baffling, but if you want to know a little more on the subject, I invite you to pursue your own research and draw your own conclusions. Personally, I have the impression that in the not-too-distant future, quantum physics may also explain why the Law of Attraction exists and reveal every single detail of how it works. Don't forget that, not very long ago, people were absolutely certain that the Earth was flat…

When you really consider it, the most powerful forces that exist are invisible to the naked eye. Love is one of the great positives forces that motivates people to go forward. Everything that we desire, do or would like to have is driven by and stems from this force. Without Love, we would literally be powerless because there would be no reason to get out of bed in the morning, to find someone to share your life with or even have children. Have you ever wondered what our world would be like without Love? To begin with, we wouldn't even exist. The forces of nature are also invisible, and yet trees grow and flowers bloom. The same is true of gravity, magnetism and air. They are invisible, yet very real – are they not? So tell me, if you believe in the existence of all these invisible forces and things, why would you doubt for a second that the Law of Attraction exists? I hope your answer isn't "because my brother-in-law told me so"! Have you noticed that the people who mock this Law don't exactly have the kind of standard of living they'd like to have? Join the people who believe that anything is possible. Having faith will made you happier, and our world will be a better place as a result. The moment you master this, you will undoubtedly say, as I did: "Ah! The vaunted Law of Attraction…"

GIVE, AND YOU SHALL AMPLY RECEIVE

(The opposite is also true).

"If you want to live happily, travel with two bags,

one to give and the other to receive."

Johann Wolfgang Von Goethe

Poet and Novelist

Does it seem paradoxical to suggest that we can receive more by giving? If you ask a cheapskate, he will probably answer that the only way to accumulate wealth is to give as little as possible and keep the maximum for yourself. Right there, we have two ways of seeing things. Which side are you on? I hope with all my heart that you are among those who believe that by giving more we receive more. And I don't mean giving the shirt off your back to the first person you see, because the word *give* can take many forms and meanings.

There are many events in our community. We're well aware of them, because every week, we receive at least one sponsorship request, and for a host of good reasons. Since we opened our businesses, I can't remember ever having turned down a single request. It's our policy to always accept in some way. The sole essential criterion is that the event be held in our community. We provide the food and drinks in most cases. Our clientele are for the most part loyal, and if they not, they soon become so. Investments like this are never a bad idea. It's no accident that both our restaurants are so busy, because we offer another highly appreciated element: impeccable customer service. We all take pride in hearing someone say that they make a detour to come to one of our two branches. And in those instances when we drop the ball, we take the time to contact the customer personally to learn more about his experience. As a result, the instance becomes an opportunity to improve ourselves. Consequently, we ensure that we will do everything in our power to see our guess back in our establishments.

People in general greatly appreciate the fact that we take the time to contact them, to apologize for the situation and to listen to what they have to say. Finally, we follow up with the employees involved to avoid a recurrence of that situation. Indeed, all the members of our team are aware that the better the service they offer, the more they receive in return. Whenever a member of the group momentarily forgets this principle for success, the others quickly remind him. I offer thanks to our entire team. Our employees also know that they can come and see us informally – they will always find a receptive ear to listen to them. We are generous with our time.

And so you've figured out **Secret number thirty-two:** be generous if you want to receive much more in return. Do you happen to be one of those people who wants to accomplish his goals at any cost, to reach the mountaintop solely to satisfy your own ego? If so, I have a confession to share with you: you will garner very little satisfaction, because the truly gratifying thing is to witness the success of those who are under your wing. Your contribution to their cause will bring you much more in return.

You can start being generous simply by giving of your time if your financial situation prevents you from doing more. It really isn't sums of money or material things that count, but sincere acts of generosity. Make this your mantra. Expect nothing in return, because life will repay you one way or another. It's as though there were a system of compensation in the universe: all that you have given will be returned to you.

And this system of compensation also works for those who spread misfortune and misery around them. You need only watch the news to understand. Week in and week out, at least one person who defrauded people for years is arrested and found guilty. Lately, dictators who ruled over their people with an iron fist for 30 years or more have become victims in turn, ending up in prison for the rest of their lives. Sooner or later, they are paid in kind. I do not agree with those who state that those people always get off scot-free with no consequences. If the justice system or a popular uprising don't take care of things, rest assured that the system of compensation will ensure that they reap, in some unexpected yet similar form or fashion, what they have sown.

So the next time you find yourself dining in a restaurant or sitting in the hairdresser's, don't hesitate to gratefully recognize the staff and their good service with a tip, secure in the knowledge that you will receive more in return.

YOUR LIFE PLAN

"Make your life a dream, and the dream a reality."

Antoine de Saint-Exupéry

Writer and poet

Do you have a Life Plan with a "To-Do" list of things to accomplish before the end of your time? Do you think that kind of planning is useless or futile? If so, the story that follows may help you experience a change of heart.

In 2005, I drew up my own list. At the time, I was on the beach in Riviera Maya in Mexico. Chantal and I were on a two-week vacation. I had brought along a new book entitled: *The Success Principles*, by popular author and motivational speaker Jack Canfield. It's an excellent book and I recommend it for anyone who has yet to make the discovery.

In two weeks, I had plenty of time to seriously dig into it. One chapter particularly struck me, addressing the importance of making a list of 100 things you would like to do during the course of your life. You would keep the list safe and sound, consulting it from time to time to remind yourself and update it. Once you'd accomplished an item, you'd put a checkmark next to it and note the date of the accomplishment date.

At the time, I wasn't sure whether or not all this would work for us, but I had decided to play along and believe that it was a tool that would produce extraordinary results. Needing 100 items for our list, we started to run out of ideas around the 75th. If this happens to you, have no fear, the penny will drop later that day or during the week. When you create this kind of list, it's only normal to wonder: "my God, if I only get a third of this done, I'll consider my life a raging success!" In fact, there's no limit to what you can write down. If you dream of traveling in outer space voyage, just enter it, without worrying about whether or not you have the means or how you will achieve it. Some items on your list will be easier to accomplish than others. Just remind yourself, you have your entire life to reach the point where you can proclaim: mission accomplished.

Seven years later, I'm happy to share with you the results of this exercise in my life. In all, we've accomplished at least 25 of the goals since then. We're talking about 25% of the total, with plenty of time ahead of us to accomplish the remaining 75. The goals we've achieved are in the travel section. Chantal and I have taken at least 50 trips all over the world since the day of the list. In fact, a number of the items accomplished involved destinations or countries that we had wanted to visit. Aside from travel, the goals include: skydiving, scuba diving, buying snowmobiles, reaching sales objectives for our business, having a luxurious property down south, etc... Other items on the list will be accomplished in the coming year. **Secret Number Thirty-Three**: planning out different things to undertake and accomplish during my time on earth. One thing that motivates me is the idea of having a parrot. I have always loved birds, and my Item Number 16 is to have a large red parrot one day. I can't wait... but the current problem is that our current residence would not suit a bird like that. That's when Chantal suggested we acquire another home down south. And so it looks like the parrot will have to wait until we live there full-time.

The truly wonderful thing would be for Chantal and I to approach the end of our lives having accomplished at least 95% of the items. Here's an important point to note: when you revise your list in two years, you may find that an item no longer suits your life at that time , because your view of things has evolved over time. In that case, you simply blot it out with Liquid Paper and add a new more suitable desire. This is also true for our list. At Number 81, I see: own a private island in the Caribbean. I'm not sure what crossed my mind on that account seven years ago, but clearly, I will have to replace it. I no longer have any desire to own a desert island. This valuable tool has worked for the thousands of people who have used it. It will also work for you, if you believe in it. So get out your Life Plan notebook and draw up your own personal list. And please be ambitious when you make your choices. I must also mention that your list need not exclusively be concerned with material goods or accomplishments, starting with To Have or To Do. You can also write down: to be a good father, if you are expecting a child, or to be a good citizen. Have fun, plan out your life, pour in a ton of dreams and imagination.

YOU ARE ALREADY RICH

"I thank God that I was born in the most beautiful country in the world."

Dany Tremblay

Entrepreneur

If you live in North America, you are very fortunate and, in fact, you are already rich compared to the rest of the world. Keep in mind that approximately 1.3 billion people on Earth live on less than one dollar a day. Furthermore, one billion people have no access to potable water. Everyone is certainly familiar with these statistics. We do not realize our incredible good fortune in having been born here instead of elsewhere.

Chantal and I have traveled practically all over the world with the exception of Asia and Africa, and have experienced many different countries and cultures. We have admired beautiful landscapes and also been able to compare the different standards of living. It is often said that comparison brings consolation, and this is certainly true as regards North Americans. The reality is striking. When you leave the resort clubs and see how the locals really live on a daily basis, you quickly realize that we are all, without exception, very rich when compared with them. We have never visited the world's poorest countries, but I would imagine the differences are even more starkly drawn. I know that there are wealth gaps in our countries as well. However, in general, unless you really want to, you don't have to walk eight kilometers to collect drinking water, or raise chickens in order to have eggs for breakfast. You just have to go to the corner grocery to find every product imaginable from the four corners of the world. And sushi lovers don't have to fly to Japan to satisfy their cravings either.

Our infrastructure is vastly superior and better adapted, and our laws better enforced. I know that things are not perfect, but in other countries, things are frightfully worse. Here, anything is possible for those with a powerful drive and ambition to succeed. Opportunity is everywhere and simply awaits for anyone to seize it. Elsewhere, opportunity is virtually nonexistent. If you do not believe me, you can always visit the village of Varadero in Cuba and you will perfectly understand what I mean. It is as if the village has been frozen in time for the past 80 years. The houses are collapsing in ruins; one swift kick would knock one over. Frankly, it's dreadful and depressing to think of the people who have to live there on. In Cuba, the inhabitants do not even have the option or opportunity to better their lot by founding their own businesses. Unfortunately, we cannot conclude that the socialist regime has been a great success for them. Capitalism has often been denounced, but the fact remains that, although imperfect, it encourages people to advance and create wealth globally.

Some tourists who traveled with us stated, seemingly to rid themselves of feelings of guilt, that the Cubans were happy, since they hadn't known any other situation and furthermore, the weather was beautiful all year 'round in their country. I do not believe that. On the contrary, I believe that the people thirst for personal freedom to fulfill their needs and desire for prosperity, not a regime in complete control of everything. Yes, we are fortunate, and we must remind ourselves often so that we never forget it. When you turn the tap, drinkable water pours forth right there in your home. You are already richer than one billion other people.

Take out your Life Plan notebook and make a list of the items you are grateful for in your life right now. I am sure there are at least twenty. If you are in good health, you should feel gratitude every day for your good fortune. Do you have a child who brings you happiness and joy? Thank life itself for that little miracle. Do you have your better half by your side? A roof over your head? A job or a business you enjoy? A car that gets you around? Etc... then thank life itself (or God) for everything it (or He) has already given you. Without exception, I perform this exercise every day during my morning shower to remind me of how fortunate I am simply to be alive. My list runs: thank you for... thank you for... and so on. As I finish up, my last item is this: thank you for raising my consciousness a little more with every passing day. In my case, I address my thanks to God, the Creator of all that is, but you can address whoever or whatever best corresponds to your beliefs. **Secret Number Thirty-Four**: recognize and be grateful what you already have, day after day. Set aside a special place within yourself for the person or thing you believe in. He will then become your guide in your personal development. As you finish your Thank You list in the shower, you will feel a state of well-being wash over you. Above all, you will realize how lucky you already are!

There is also another exercise you absolutely must work up in your Life Plan notebook. Make a list of all the things you have already accomplished in your life up to that point. When making my own list, I was hugely impressed by its length. Start from your earliest childhood. Did you learn how to walk? Mark it down in your list, and so on… Did you learn how to talk? To read? Play baseball? Skate? Did you graduate from high school? University? Can you speak Spanish? Were you ever named volunteer of the year in your community? Etc… Don't leave anything out! You will recognize how spectacularly accomplished you have been throughout all that time. That is **Secret Number Thirty-Five**: we have all been worthy and incredible right up to this point, and since our Day Number One on the planet. The preceding exercises are intended to pump up your confidence. When your confidence is unwavering, anything is possible, without exception. Unfortunately, most people have a poor self-image, when quite the opposite should be true. Stop running yourself down in your own mind, telling yourself you are worthless, because nothing could be further from the truth. From now on, you must congratulate yourself, and be good to yourself – not only for who and what you are, but also for what you have already accomplished. That's an order I'm giving you, not a choice. Only at that very moment can you tell yourself in all sincerity that you are already rich.

MEASURING UP

"The glory of great men should always be measured by the means they have used to acquire it."

La Rochefoucauld

Writer and Moralist

This next chapter will genuinely help you propel yourself forward if you have the courage required to perform the exercise as it will be described to you below. It demands a bit of effort on your part. However, as you know, nothing in this world is gained without effort. Every aspect of your life that you wish to improve must be measured in order for you to know where you are right now and what the goal is at the finish line. This is **Secret Number Thirty-Six**: everything that must be improved must also be monitored and measured on a regular basis.

Here is a perfect example: the Olympic Games. Whether it's the hundred-meter dash or the pole vault, you'll surely agree that the winner is the athlete who has the fastest time or the highest vault, right? Now do you think that the event judges use their eagle eyes to determine the winners? Of course not. They use various tools including a stopwatch timed to the milliseconds, as well as video replay and laser-photo sequences. In short, many techniques and technologies are used to measure where each competitor ranks.

Now let's look at the athletes. As you know, all athletes spend hours training every day for years and years before the Games are held. Do you truly believe that during training sessions these athletes run or swim without measuring their performance, thinking: measuring this isn't important, because I know I can run/swim fast? That would be a recipe for disaster! In fact, they time/measure each and every race to gauge their progress and keep meticulous statistics to compare training sessions. If you really want to attain financial freedom or even become a millionaire one day, you must do as the athletes do and measure your progress frequently throughout the year. A simple tool Chantal and I have used for years now is the "Excel" computer file to measure our net worth. Net worth is the amount that determines what would be left in our pockets tomorrow morning if we were to sell everything we owned, in addition to paying back all of our debts (value of our assets minus our debts).

At the very top of your file, begin by writing down the value of all of your assets line by line as follows: First, write down the current market value of your property. If you don't know it, seek out similar properties for sale in your neighborhood – or do what we did and simply call a qualified real estate agent, who will write up a detailed evaluation. Next, in the lines beneath, write out the current value of your vehicles, the approximate value of your furnishings and the other objects in your home. On the conservative side, since these belongings are used. Then, write down the current value of all your investments, the approximate combined amount in your bank accounts, etc... At the end of your list, add up all the amounts and write the figure under: "Total Assets."

Next, conduct the same exercise a few lines lower for your debts, as follows: average balance on your credit cards, mortgage balance, balance on your automobile loans, student loan, unpaid government income tax (which I hope is 'zero'!). finally, when you've finished, add up the figures under: "Total Debts." To complete the exercise, write on the last line: "Net worth," which is the sum of your assets minus the sum of your debts. If you've never drawn up such file before, I understand the concern or worry you may feel in finding out the result of this accounting exercise. Don't forget, though, that this is a tool facilitating self-improvement. Since we've been using this tool, the growth curve of our net worth has been exponential.

Ideally, every two months, make any necessary corrections to your file as the amounts change. Only note changes to those items that vary significantly; the value of your investments is a good example. The value of your home or your furnishings will not vary greatly in the course of two months. Only make a correction in that section once every year, or perhaps even two years. Don't forget that, little by little, the balance of your loans will decrease pas. You will have to update them as well. Also remember that each year, the value of our vehicles depreciates. Use the *Canadian Black Book* or the *Kelley Blue Book* as a reference point. If your vehicles are leased, do not add anything to your assets column, because the cars do not belong to you. I can practically see your face going white as a sheet. You probably dread that this exercise will be long and tiresome, don't you? You could not be further from the truth. Updating your file will take about 5 minutes every 2 months. All you need to do is take out your bankcard and visit your online financial profile. Everything is right there: the value of your investments, the balances of your bank accounts, loans, etc… In fact, the longest part of the exercise is drawing up your file in the first place. It takes one hour, and the rest is easy as pie.

Write the current year in your file and when you're done, make a photocopy for safekeeping. After several years have passed, you will observe your progress by making comparisons between them. You can also draw up a chart or graph every year to reveal your progress. We have done it, and suggest you do as well, because it offers a very gratifying visual. These tools will clearly show you whether or not you are heading in the right direction. One day, a friend whom I had begun to mentor shared his despair over his financial situation. In just a few minutes, I had succeeded in convincing him to do the exercise together in order to take a closer look at his situation. His liquidity was indeed relatively low ($0 in his bank account…). I understood why he was depressed. However, at the end of the exercise, his net worth came out to be over $224,000, largely thanks to the value of his investments and the value of his house in relation to his mortgage balance. I had succeeded in boosting his morale in no time, thanks to this exercise. I followed by advising him to cut up his credit card and aggressively pay off its balance, because with its 18% interest rate, it was clearly the cause of his problem. How should we define the term "being a millionaire"? Most people are under the misconception that being a millionaire means having 1 million dollars in the bank. I must share my opinion on the subject with you: having 1 million dollars in the bank generating 0% in interest is not very intelligent. There are better ways to make your capital grow, and we will explore them in the upcoming chapters. To me, being a millionaire means having 1 million dollars in "<u>net worth</u>". And there is only one method that will reveal whether you have that much-vaunted million dollars in net worth: you must measure your finances using the file as described in this chapter. And so, I have one question for you, dear reader: as you read these lines, do you exactly know your net worth?

ACQUIRING ASSETS

"Wealth, power and all that men most value, is in reality worthless but for the satisfaction of giving them up."

Leo Tolstoy

Russian author

The speed with which you acquire assets paves the way to financial freedom. And here, the word "asset" must be properly defined. We will therefore take our time in dissecting and analyzing it to avoid any confusion. People use that word in every which way, but in our book, there is no grey area. That is **Secret Number Thirty-Seven**: acquiring assets will absolutely build your wealth. An asset is an investment that makes you richer on a regular basis. Here are some examples: our two restaurants are assets, because they generate profits, which in turn enrich us. A job is an asset because it generates income, which in turn enriches the jobholder every time he collects his paycheck.

A rental property is an asset only if its revenue exceeds all of its expenses. In this case, the difference between the two is equal to positive cash flow. Positive cash flow enriches the property owner, and is therefore considered an asset. When a property's cash flow is negative (expenses higher than revenue), the missing amount must be paid out by the property holder to cover the shortfall. In this case, the property impoverishes the owner. The property is therefore considered a burden rather than an asset.

This type of situation arises when the property owner has paid too much for the building, or underestimated his current expenditures. It may also arise because some of the units are vacant. In this case, all is not lost: you must simply attract new tenants and the property can then be moved into the assets category. "You" and "your decisions" are what ensure whether or not your rental investment is an asset. If you are a good property manager, you can probably succeed in making sure that your property is 100% leased. Some people dispute my way of grading assets. I respect their opinion, especially because the sale of the property may bring a capital gain (profit), against the purchase price. I respond that this criticism represents a purely speculative hypothesis because nobody can predict the future with absolute accuracy. Real estate is in no way immune to a generalized drop in prices. That's why I advise investors looking to get involved in rental property to base their purchase criteria on the cash flow rather than on possible sales profit. All the better if there is a profit upon sale – that's a bonus, as they say. In the meantime, you must avoid having to bear the financial burden of the property in question.

The same logic applies to financial products: a guaranteed investment certificate is an asset because it produces interest revenue, however low it may be. Do you now understand what I mean by an asset? Next, spend five minutes making a list of all the assets you currently hold. If you have included your car, please re-read the preceding paragraph from the beginning. A car is a consumer good that, far from making you wealthy, must be seen for what it is: one of the worst products there is on a financial level, although I understand that they are very useful in your daily life.

Let us continue. Have you included your personal residence in your list? Once again, in our opinion, that is a mistake. A home is a choice, or a lifestyle is you prefer. The difference compared to an automobile is that the purchase price will tend to follow the inflation rate rather than depreciate over the years. Has your home already generated revenue since you purchased it? If you answered no, that's probably because you and your family live in it. You will have to get up every morning and work hard for decades in order to pay the bills and the mortgage.

And guess what? When the house has been paid off in twenty-five years, it will be high time to renovate and bring it up to date, especially if you never did so along the way. You will of course respond that a person has to live somewhere. You are right. Is it better to pay rent all your life or to have a place of your own? That's up to you to decide, and your lifestyle will furnish the answer. I simply want to show you that if your personal residence does not generate any revenue, it should not be considered an asset that is productive in that sense of the term. And so you can likely see that a personal residence will not fill your pockets with money. Do you want solid proof? Check the account books of the bank that is financing your mortgage. You will discover that your personal residence is listed in their "assets" column. In accounting, the same asset cannot be considered as such in two different ledgers. In other words, your house cannot be considered a bank asset and your personal asset at the same time. An asset to one becomes a liability to the other. Thus, the bank holds the asset because you are the one who sends them monthly mortgage payments. As a result, they collect revenue every month, to their profit. Your house becomes your liability as long as you make monthly payments and your mortgage loan remains in force.

You will now tell me that one day, it will be fully paid down. That's true, but even so, it will never be an asset, because you will still have to pay municipal taxes, school taxes, the electric bill, landscaping and renovations one day or another, which will probably require another bank loan. The bank will be very happy to give you this new "renovation" loan and collect on its asset for years more to come! There is another element to clarify. Your house is not really yours while you have a mortgage or bank lien. Just try not paying your mortgage loan or municipal taxes for a few months and you'll see what I mean. Your land isn't exactly yours either. If you discover a cache of gold in the ground, you'll soon be informed that your lawn belongs to the state. But please don't shoot the messenger.

I am not calling into question your decision to have purchased your own home, if you have done so. We also have our own cozy residence and have loved it for years. The sole point I want to share with you is that we see it as a life choice rather than an asset. As I have stated, our house does not produce any revenue for us. It tends to hold its purchase price against inflation, but it does not enrich us on a daily basis. However, if you do not have the discipline to save systematically in your day-to-day life, owning your own home is probably advisable, since it will force you to do so as a result.

Ouch! The worst is over, and I hope you're not too angry at me. I believe we've got to call a spade a spade. So, if you are following view of assets, what's left on your list? Perhaps a registered retirement savings plan? I think this type of retirement plan can be a very good asset because it encourages saving. Also, the growth of your capital is sheltered from taxation for a number of years. And when we say long-term, you've got a major ally in your corner: compound return, year after year. I think most people are very familiar with this concept.

For those who've never heard of it, this means your money produces a return from the very start; which in turn generates further returns every year, and so on after that. It's a little like a snowball effect. Time does its work and thereby becomes your best friend. And that is precisely why we are so strongly advised to start a retirement savings plan as early as possible.

CELEBRATE YOUR VICTORIES

A faith worthy of celebration can

remake the world

John-Paul II

Pope

Is there anything in life better than pleasure? Playing games, school recess and the holidays would certainly rank as some of your fondest childhood memories. When looking back on these events, have you ever noticed that you only occasionally remember what people said at the time? On the other hand, we always clearly remember having felt good or having had fun. Pleasure is an integral part of my life. I try to have a good time in everything I undertake. Life is much more entertaining that way. When I was a child, I was drawn to anything that was fun and repelled by anything that seemed dreary. I still have that modus operandi today, and I never want to stray from it as long as I live. I never surround myself with demoralizing people who have forgotten how to laugh and have a good time. If I do not enjoy doing something, I don't do it, no matter what other people may think about that. I believe that if I feel good in my own skin, those around me will sense that and feel good in my presence. It's contagious, as they say, and that is my mantra. Even if I am with people in a meeting to discuss serious matters, I ensure that everything unfolds in a relaxed atmosphere filled with laughter and camaraderie. The results are 100 times better and the messages I want to communicate messages go down much more easily. Over time, Chantal and I have developed the tradition of buying a bottle of champagne whenever we acquire a new property or accomplish one of our goals. After having popped the cork, we make a toast to officially celebrate the event. Immediately afterwards, we inscribe the date and a description of the goal on the cork. We've carefully stored the corks in our library for the past 4 years. As I write these lines, there are at least 18 of them, each representing a different goal we've accomplished. That's our little "success collection." From time to time, we check on them to remind ourselves of what we've accomplished. We are always a little surprised at how many of them we have.

Memory has a way of fading, and you can forget what you have accomplished. That is **Secret Number Thirty-Eight**: celebrate all of your victories and you will certainly remember them.

YOUR CONSUMER HABITS

"Consume the consumer society."

Denis Langlois

Author

What kind of consumer are you? Do you try to impress others with your lifestyle? I recently read an article mentioning that in China, the newly emerging middle class is more interested in appearing wealthy than in truly becoming so. I am not surprised, because we can also observe the same phenomenon here.

They want to appear better-off than their neighbor. Members of this group share some common factors: they are educated and intelligent. They have a high-paying job, let's say with an annual salary of $60,000 or more. They have this year's model car in the driveway, a large home that exceeds their real needs, and travel every year, etc... They work hard their entire lives, often to find themselves exactly where they were when they started, without a penny in their pockets. Most of the time they end up riddled with debt, meaning they're worse off than when they began. I'll admit that at first glance, they appear very comfortable, but there is often nothing behind the curtain. If you are among those who think this way, you must get a hold of yourself, because ultimately, your life will end up being an experience in pure consumption. Like a flame that consumes and ends up in a pile of ashes, you will build nothing of value. I am not saying that consumption is bad – quite the opposite. I am simply stating that this is not the right path to take as you start out. The ideal method is to build a solid foundation, like a profitable business or a real estate portfolio, which will generate an inflow of income every month. Then, with your new sources of monthly revenue, you can consume and enjoy your life as you see fit.

My spouse and I have traveled a lot. However, we did not do so before we had acquired our business. And after we had, we poured two more years of effort into making it solid and profitable. Only in the third year did we leave our tiny apartment, by our home and then finally begin to travel. I have noticed that many little things you can do in life can save you thousands of dollars for essentially the same experience. It starts with travel. There are a number of websites offering prices that can vary widely. Our last trip was to Florida. Simply by switching airline companies, we were able to save $900. Also, when you travel during the week, say on a Wednesday, prices can vary by as much as $300 to $600. Cancellation insurance is an expensive add-on that we never sign up for. We take the risk because we think it is minimal. Up until now, that decision has been very beneficial. I am aware that the insurance may be very useful for certain types of people, like the elderly.

Wine is also a very particular commercial sector. We enjoy drinking red wine during family gatherings, or with a good meal. I have noticed that the price of wine is not always set in relation to the quality or flavor as such. Every individual has very personal tastes. My own tasting experience illustrated that the optimal price range in terms of quality for money was in the $14 -$18 range per bottle (which is, of course, my opinion). After buying several bottles in the $30 to $50 price range, we realized that our palates were not expert enough to appreciate the difference between the two product ranges – and that this was not our goal, in any case. Some bottles are more expensive simply because they are popular and have name-brand recognition.

Champagne, which is in fact just bubbly white wine, is another good example. The name "Champagne" refers to the region in France. Foreign producers of sparkling wines are therefore not permitted to use that name. The producers of Champagne therefore profit from the reputation of the name in selling products at what we believe is an inflated price. I recently tried a sparkling wine from Spain, and enjoyed it. The difference: rather than paying $50 for the bottle, it cost us $16. Once again, I am no expert in sparkling wines, but I could not tell the difference, except in my wallet. I advise you not to be hoodwinked by brand names and purchase according to your own taste experience. The clothing industry is another intelligent business to be in. Just by stitching a tiny logo on a garment, a company can quadruple or quintuple its price. A cotton sweater that cost $2 to make in Asia can easily retail for $60 on our store shelves with some tiny logo on it. I don't want come across as though I never buy anything – on the contrary, my clothing comes from Italy and costs thousands of dollars when I shop. The difference is that I have the means to do so, which is not necessarily the case for all fans of designer fashions.

Do you automatically shop around when you receive your annual home or automobile insurance renewal? I advise you to do so, and call at least three new insurance companies every year. To this point, I've never saved less than $200. My philosophy, and **Secret Number Thirty-Nine** is: the price is always too high and you must always find something better for less. Buying a car is another area in which you can make major savings. Last year, Chantal and I bought a well-appointed Volvo XC90 SUV. Brand new, the vehicle retailed for around $70,000, plus 16% in sales tax. We found the model and color we wanted in a year-old SUV with 15,000 km on the odometer. We picked up this fabulous roadster for $44,000 plus 9% in sales tax, given it was a used car. You can clearly see the mindset to adopt. I strongly advise you to adapt this strategy and purchase vehicles from the previous model year. Let others pay for thousands of dollars in depreciation.

If you're looking to buy a previously-owned home, make an offer far lower than the asking price, even if your real estate broker does not agree. If he insists, change brokers, because after all, you are the one paying. Do not be led by your sentiments, be firm in your approach and it will translate into thousands of dollars in savings. Then, have the property inspected and the cost of all necessary repairs evaluated by a trusted renovation contractor. Come back with a detailed list and propose that the seller make the necessary repairs himself or lower the price of the property by the amount of the repair estimate. Leave nothing to chance, approaching the project as though you were a businessman or businesswoman. Furthermore, by paying your mortgage every two weeks instead of monthly, you can shorten the term and end up paying off your house four years earlier on a 25-year mortgage. Did you know that this could amount to thousands of dollars in interest savings?

Last year, I called my bank manager and told him his fees were too high. In the final analysis, he had two choices: lose me as a client, or surrender. He surrendered, and I was able to save $300 in current fees. Not bad for a 5 minute phone call. Do likewise, because if you don't ask, you'll get nothing in return. Is your mortgage too expensive? Analyze what the competition can offer you and charge ahead any time you can gain from a change. Last year, I discovered that there was a new home telephone option, a device called "magicJack" that connects to the Internet. You can then make toll-free calls all over North America, all for $10 per year. I took the leap and now pocket a permanent saving of $400 every year. Since then, my parents and my brother have followed suit as well and are very happy to deprive the big telephone company of that money.

When you shop for groceries, do you compare prices? Sometimes, an equivalent product can be found for $1 less. I know it's only a dollar. It's not the amount that matters but the frequency with which you do this. How many grocery store items will you need in your lifetime? Thousands upon thousands? If you aren't careful, you will have wasted tens of thousands of dollars in the final analysis. If you truly want to become rich, then firmly tell yourself one thing: every little dollar counts. And when you see a penny lying on the sidewalk, bend down and pick it up. It is a sign of respect, proclaiming to the spirit of Infinite Wealth: You're always welcome in my home!

HOW IS YOUR ARMY DOING?

"Having pity for one's enemy means having

no pity for oneself."

Francis Bacon

Philosopher

If there's one book that should definitely be on your gift list, it is *The Richest Man in Babylon*. The book features a concept that left a permanent impression on me. It advises you to think of every dollar you have as a soldier in your service. Your full tally of soldiers makes up your army. Do you like the analogy? I think it's brilliant. Like an army, when it heads to the battlefront, it can defeat other soldiers. Unfortunately, if you send your battalion our blindly, you may never see it again, or it may return reduced in number by half. Does that seem like a grade-school metaphor to you? I assure you that it is not. It precisely reflects reality. When an investment opportunity becomes available, your job is to analyze the booby-traps on the battlefield (revenue and expenses, inherent risks, etc...). Next, it is important to have a Plan B in case events do not unfold as intended. If you've done your homework properly, you can enjoy the victory and watch as your soldiers return in greater number than they were in at the start. If the unexpected occurs along the way, your Plan B is in place ready to take over.

A similar situation recently cropped up for my father and me. An investment opportunity became available to us last year. It involved building a round, wooden three-storey Scandinavian style house on a one-acre lot along a river. The land was in a posh town in the Laurentians. We did our research and due diligence, and realized that there was only one comparable house on the market and that we had the opportunity to build the equivalent for hundreds of thousands of dollars less. Our Plan A was to build and sell the property speedily and cash in a quick profit. Plan B was to hold on to the property and rent it out. The rental market for that type of property was over $2000 per month – not an inconsiderable amount. The result, after construction, was spectacular, with the added bonus of a huge sauna on the land. However, during construction, the market for vacation properties experienced something of a lull, something rarely seen in the region.

As arranged, we moved on to Plan B and rented the property very quickly for $2200 per month. Our soldiers were not in danger for the moment. On the contrary, they sent us new soldiers every month thanks to the rental. However, full repatriation of the troops will take longer than expected. The same principle may apply when you go to Wal-Mart and they have a new product on the market which is perfectly useless to your life, but with nonetheless captures your full attention. When this occurs in your future, think of your poor defenseless soldiers, whom you are marching off to certain death! And so, I ask you the following: how is your army doing? Is it expanding, stagnating, or far worse, getting smaller?

NUTRITION

"Let food be thy medicine and medicine be thy food."

Hippocrates

Philosopher

I still do not know your plans for the future, but I do know one thing. If you wish to accomplish your ambitions, you will need a healthy dose of energy. In general, does your nutrition adhere to the adage: a healthy mind in a healthy body? Do you make the right choices? There is a category of people in our society who live in complete denial. When they discuss their diet, everything seems to be going well and all is clear in their minds. However, when you compare their words and actions, you find contradictions.

Over the past twelve years, our diet has evolved a great deal. When I met my spouse, we would sometimes eat out at Chinese buffets. Helping myself to four servings of dessert during those evenings was the norm rather than the exception. My in-laws simply could not believe what they were seeing. I was also renowned for my appetite for cherry cheesecake. I would request it for every birthday. I was in my twenties, and my slim physique afforded my every imaginable excess. However, during the week, I would not overindulge. We also went to fast food restaurants, like everyone else.

Today, those who know us find us a little strange, and I understand why. We eat differently from most people. Perforce, in our society, anything different is considered a little bizarre. We haven't eaten potatoes, fries, boiled or mashed, for over three years. We no longer eat rice. It's rare for us to eat more than 2 servings of bread in the course of a day. Cheese is virtually nonexistent in our diet. We drink soy milk and in my case, dairy products no longer factor in my menu. We no longer eat desserts. We've also abandoned fast food restaurants, aside from our chain, because it is one of the few to offer healthy options that are in harmony with out choices. Our meats are all grilled, and fried foods are not part of our day-to-day life. We haven't reduced our cheese consumption because we don't like the taste, but because it is so hard to digest and extremely high in fat.

Wow – we certainly have turned into space aliens, haven't we? I respect your opinion and am not asking you to follow our lifestyle choices. Our meals consist of: meats and plenty of vegetables and salads. I am fortunate, because Chantal is probably the world champion of salads, and also makes all her own vinaigrettes (with no preservatives or chemical products).

We are fans of fish and seafood. We also like Italian cuisine and pasta. In the morning, we always eat a wide variety of fresh fruits, and healthy cereals, especially multigrain Cheerios. Don't bother looking for soft drinks in our fridge because they've all expired; we prefer a nice glass of wine instead. All of this did not happen in one go. Rather, it was the result of experiences we tried and enjoyed. In fact, it all started six years ago. We were curious to know if we were capable of giving up dessert on a permanent basis. We extended the experiment over the course of a month and discovered that it was not difficult. We did not miss dessert. We were surprised ourselves by the result and then naturally decided to make this our mantra. The principle was as follows: desserts were not banned. On the contrary, they were permitted at any time. We simply decided on them from day to day. When a birthday comes along, we sometimes enjoy a small slice of cake, for the sake of our guests more than ourselves.

Then, three years later, Chantal read a book on the Montignac Method. Once again she proposed that we attempt a new experiment. Her question: what would our meals be like without potatoes and rice? I suggested that we try that for a week. Once again, the experience was surprising. We found that we ate far more vegetables, other than potatoes, and a lot more salad. We also enjoyed the effect that this had on our systems. Upon waking in the morning, we felt a sensation of physical lightness and well-being. We so greatly enjoyed the experience that since then, we have adopted it indefinitely. The principles were clear from the outset: if we grow tired with the choice someday, we will simply drop it. And also, nothing is forbidden. Once or twice a year when we go to a Japanese restaurant, we enjoy a bit of rice. Strangely, our stomachs become swollen and congested almost immediately.

Chantal has a recipe for coquilles St-Jacques that everyone just loves. There is a bit of potato in the dish. Do we go without it? Not on your life. As I've been saying, this is a choice made on a regular basis rather than a law against certain foods. Another advantage in eschewing potatoes is that it automatically keeps us far away from fast food restaurants. Have you ever gone into a fast food joint to only eat a hamburger with a glass of water?

One of our great pleasures in healthy eating is in avoiding processed foods. Take ready-to-eat lasagnas you buy from the grocery store. While they are indeed tasty, their list of ingredients is worrisome. Read the unknown, unpronounceable names and they will make you think twice. If you want to make permanent changes in your eating habits, follow **Secret Number Forty**: you must deeply enjoy the changes you make. Try it out for a week or two. If you find the change difficult or unpleasant, that's a sign that you must step back. You will never succeed in your approach if you take no pleasure from it. Never forget that your brain is stronger than your reason. When the brain takes no pleasure in making a new change, it tries everything to convince your reason to retreat. The brain is patient and knows that it will win out over la raison thanks to the strategy of erosion. It's a little like a child who wants something and repeats it over and over until the parent cracks. That's precisely why all diets are destined to fail. Your brain takes no pleasure from them and as a result wages a merciless battle against your reason.

Our success is explained by the fact that we fell in love with out nutritional lifestyle. I understand that healthy eating habits are not necessarily the same for everyone. Everyone has his or her own vision and opinion on them. I do not purport to have the absolute truth on the subject. All I can tell you is that it worked for us, and that we find it very fulfilling. And so, assess your situation and see if certain changes can match up enjoyably   with   your   lifestyle.

BRICK AND MORTAR

"Real estate cannot be lost or stolen,

nor can it be taken away. Purchased with common sense,

paid for in full, and managed with reasonable care,

it is about the safest investment in the world."

Franklin D. Roosevelt

President of the United States

Do you like real estate? It is often said that property is a rock-solid investment. This is true, in particular in certain product categories. During my last visit to Toronto, the skyline was full of building condo towers, each more attractive than the last. I sincerely believe that those who want to acquire this type of top-end product expose themselves to a financial risk. As far as I'm concerned, this type of boom is a bad sign. Indeed, when I notice this irrational phenomenon, I know that I'm witnessing real estate speculation, which will end badly eventually. Personally, we stay very, very far away from that kind of product. I doubt it's a good investment, if renting out this type of real estate purchase cannot possibly generate positive cash flow. Real estate is what we love most, after being business people. The challenge when you begin to reap major sums from your business is to make that money work anew for you. It's generally a bad decision to leave your loot sleeping uselessly in the bank. There are a number of options to make your money work more effectively, including real estate. When I discuss investing in real estate, I mean properties that produce rental income, and not a second weekend home by the lake. It's lovely to have a chalet where you can while away the holidays, but in this instance, it's much more a luxurious lifestyle choice than an investment as far as I'm concerned.

For two years now, Chantal and I have been particularly active in the American real estate market. Why there? We find the Canadian real estate market too expensive for our tastes, and the good opportunities are few and far between. The trigger point occurred when the property sector in Arizona dropped like a stone in 2009. We had previously visited and fallen in love with the region, as we love to play golf. When the news reached its worst point, we decided the time was right to leap onto the available opportunities.

Several weeks later, we acquired a property in a Phoenix suburb for $60,000. The house was owned by the bank, which had foreclosed on it. Built in 2003, it has 3 bedrooms and 2 bathrooms, with a double garage. A similar property in Canada retails in the $275,000 range. This property had sold new for $180,000. We told ourselves it was impossible to go wrong with a price so ridiculously low. One month later there was a permanent tenant in the house, who lives there still. His monthly rent is $800. The beauty of the situation is that taxes are so low that we bank almost all of the rental income. Since then, we have acquired over ten other properties including a quadruplex. They are all rented out year-'round. Our frequency of purchase is approximately one property every 3 months. Our goal is to have about fifty properties in our portfolio soon. **Secret Number Forty-One**: put your money to work in rental property in the U.S. Recently, we have also begun to help people like us acquire rental properties at sales pieces on the U.S. market. We guide them through the process from start to finish. Here is our modus operandi for investing with success. Some gurus would charge you hundreds of dollars to attend a seminar that will show you the very same things.

First, the purchase location is important. If your choice ends up being in a disreputable neighborhood or a city with no future, you will bitterly regret it. We very much like the Phoenix area in Arizona. The city has experienced unrivalled price drops in recent years. In addition, if we look into the future a bit, we can predict without going to far out on a limb that retired Baby Boomers from the northern states of the U.S. will want to move there permanently. That includes a fair number of Canadians for six months of the year. We therefore think that there will be sustained demand in the years to come. The city has a hot and dry climate and the cost of living is really affordable. It has nothing in common with California.

We also want to invest in the city of Charlotte in North Carolina for somewhat similar reasons, but in particular because the city's economy seems solid and resilient. Florida is the third state, specifically the West Palm Beach area, where we already invest but to a lesser extent, because in Florida the monthly communal association fees of gated communities are higher, as are insurance fees. These two factors chip away a good bit of monthly rental income. There are other interesting cities on our preferred list: Memphis (Tennessee), San Antonio (Texas), Las Vegas (Nevada), Atlanta (Georgia).

We try to acquire foreclosed properties owned by banks. There are plenty to choose from and the prices are very affordable. And can you believe that we have never seen any of our properties in person? You read that right. We use a number of Internet tools in making our investment decisions. The first is a popular site: www.realtor.com, a good place to begin your research. You must however realize that the best opportunities are snapped up quickly and that a property you find attractive may no longer be available. The "Speedy Gonzales" types of this world are the ones who are most successful in this type of market. One good way to give yourself an advantage against the competition is to program an automatic notification into your computer to alert you immediately when a new property lands on the market. You can then level the playing field against "Speedy Gonzales." It is not uncommon to see a number of offers submitted for the same property at the same time. If you only bid up to the asking price, there is slim chance that your offer will be accepted. The property will be granted to the highest bidder. When we first submit an offer on a property held by the bank, we always bid the full asking price. If we are the sole bidders, the offer is generally accepted as is. If there are a number of offers at the same time, we shift our price four to five thousand dollars higher. Sometimes we win, sometimes we don't.

One criterion we look for involves properties with an asking price three times lower than during the 2006 speculation era, at the height of the real estate bubble. If, for example, a property is listed at $55,000, you can verify all the details at www.zillow.com Enter the address of the property. When you view the property dossier, you will find a graph illustrating the property value over the past 10 years. If you check the year 2006 and the graph reveals that the property had a value of $165,000 or more, you are potentially looking at a good catch. Furthermore, the graph will indicate if the property has been sold during the past 10 years. If so, you'll find out when the transaction occurred, and the price.

The file will also indicate how much you can ask for in monthly rent if you decide to go that way. If the possible rent has a ratio between 5 and 8 compare to the asking price, you are practically assured of a good return on your investment. For example: you're looking at a property with an asking price of $60,000 and you can ask for $850 in monthly rent, or $10,200 per year. To figure out the price ratio in relation to rent, take the asking price ($60,000) and divide it by the annual rent ($10,200). Your ration is therefore ratio 5.88, which is excellent. This quick and simple method will save you time and help you make a sound decision.

If you want further info on projected rent, there is also a specialized website called www.rentometer.com Enter the address of the property, and then indicate the number of rooms in the dwelling and the amount of rent you want from your future tenant. Let us say for illustration purposes that you enter $900 per month. Hit "Analyze My Rent" and if the needle dial indicates "green," you'll know that the monthly amount is a complete bargain for the tenant. Yellow indicates that the rent is average for the area, and red indicates it is excessive. The system will also supply a map with all the rents presently in force in that neighborhood, indicating the amount of each.

Once a monthly rent has been established in accordance with the market, it is time to calculate to find out if your investment will provide an acceptable return. Before we continue, it is important to inform Canadian investors that you must pay for your property in cash. In most cases, an American bank will not offer you financing. The best method is to use the available equity on your house in Canada to pay for properties in the U.S. Now let us continue with the return. Begin by calculating the annual revenue provided by the property. Let's take the real example of one of our properties located in Charlotte in North Carolina. At $900 in monthly rent, it generates $10,800 in annual revenue. Next come the expenses: annual tax of $954 (you can find out the annual taxes on each of the properties you're aiming for at www.zillow.com). Insurance costs $641 per year, maintenance and repairs approximately $800 (I generally use that amount), property management costs $900 annually. The remaining costs are assumed by the tenant, including electricity, heating, etc…

Therefore, our total annual costs amount to $3295. The purchase price of the house was $55,000, plus $5000 in varied costs to bring the house up to rental standards, $750 in notary fees and finally $500 for inspection fees. That brings us to a total acquisition cost of $61,250 for the property. The amount left to us after having paid expenses is $7505 (total revenue minus expenses). To find out your return, you must divide $7505 by $61,250 and multiply the total by 100. In our case, our annual return on this investment is 12.26%. Just try and show me an investment that can provide you with a return on your capital as high as that (and year after year)! And the best part of the story, which I have not accounted for, is that five years from now, the value of the property may have doubled. We can't be certain about that, of course.

Do not put too much trust in photographs when looking for a potential investment, especially when it involves a bank seizure, because that will mean the people who lived there previously have endured a bank foreclosure. As a result, they may not have left it in impeccable condition. As a general rule, if you like the exterior of the dwelling, prospective tenants are likely to think along the same lines.

As regards the interior, we hold the following criteria: if the inspection report indicates that the place needs a new coat of paint, the carpeting must be replaced and that some other modifications are required, we forge ahead, considering these to be minor renovations. If the walls are full of holes and the cabinets are mangled, we give up on it and look for another.

You must be especially careful when dealing with a property built before the '90s, because they can often harbor a multitude of unexpected problems. We witnessed just that during a purchase offer on a property in Ohio. It was built in 1940 and seemed well-preserved for its age. The price was $25,000, and so we thought it looked like a great opportunity. Our opinion changed when we received the inspection report. There were at least 75 pages of problems! Needless to say, we turned it down. We learn by trying and doing. As a result, we decided that we would not make any future offers on older properties. Our time is very valuable, and we are investors, not renovators.

Now let us move on to the next elements to check up on: the neighborhood. If there are any abandoned houses or slums in the area, you would want to know, right? We like to use a very helpful tool called Google Street View. First, go to the Google Maps website. Then, enter the address of the property and you will have a number of viewing options for the building. We find the best to be "Street View," because it allows you to move about on the street(s) of the area as though you were taking a stroll after dinner! You'll gain a foretaste of your future neighbors and of the area in general. For much more technical data on the neighborhood, visit: www.homefacts.com Enter the address of the property and you will have all the information you need to make a more enlightened decision. The data will include everything from the nearest police station to the likelihood of tornados or earthquakes in the area. One element we like to know is the city crime rate. An assigned rating of 100 indicated the national average in the U.S. A rating of 245 indicates that the actual crime rate in the neighborhood is far above the average. You can even check up on any murders committed in the area, and the reasons behind them. If there is any known ground contamination, the map will indicate its location in relation to the building. Another important indicator is the average annual household income in that community. You can find out if the area is poor by verifying if it has an abnormally low average annual household income.

The unemployment rate is also listed, which is very important as well. We have no interest in investing in a city like Detroit where the unemployment rate is 20%. Sure, the houses are practically free, but that's because that's all they're worth. A high unemployment rate often spurs a population exodus. A population exodus means much lower housing demand, lower rents or property that remains empty for long periods, none of which is positive. There is another site worth mentioning: Sperling's Best Places Real Estate (www.bestplaces.net/). Enter the name of the city where you would like to invest. Among other data, you can discover if future demographic trends for the city are positive or negative. You can also compare cities and their respective positive and negative aspects. The site even has a blog where people offer their personal opinions. In short, it's an essential online destination for information on trends and helps clarify your thinking.

Do you enjoy websites that allow you to chat with like-minded people who share your interests? If so, I have the perfect site for you when it comes to real estate issues. I advise you to join the BiggerPockets community at www.biggerpockets.com This site allows you to discuss issues and ask pertinent questions on a host of subjects. People on the site are very generous with their time and will answer anything you want to know. To give you an idea, there are currently 100,000 active members on this social network site specializing in real estate. Once a property passes the test and meets the majority of your criteria, it is time to make an offer. Oh yes! I must inform you that it is normal to discover that not all of your criteria will be met. If you wait for everything to be perfect, you may end up waiting an awful long time.

To make an offer, you must have a team in place working in concert with you. It is essential to build a strong relationship with a real estate agent who understands your needs. When you contact an agent for the first time, make sure you seriously intend to acquire property – if not, don't waste his or her time. Real estate agents cannot stand window-shoppers. If that's your approach, you'll swiftly be ignored and will have to start the process of building a solid and lasting relationship from scratch. Having a real estate agent on the ground is vitally important, because he will save you time by sending you available property lists that correspond to your criteria, which simply await your purchase offer, and cannot necessarily be found on general websites. Don't forget that there is a considerable inventory of bank-owned properties that must be liquidated (4 million of them, as I write these lines). They do not always have the means to put those properties on the real estate market, as is the case with other products in a normal market. The best opportunities won't be found on TV or in the news! Your agent will guide you through the questions surrounding the purchase offer. However, I want to warn you about the purchase conditions when dealing with bank-owned properties; and you will feel somewhat uncomfortable when you first read this. In every case, the property must be purchased as is, thus weighting the contract heavily in the bank's favor. You cannot alter a thing. That is the normal process with bank seizures. If your offer is indeed accepted by the bank, congratulations! However, do not waste a minute before calling an inspection company, because you will only have 7 days, including weekends, to declare yourself satisfied or to withdraw.

You may be wondering who manages our real estate portfolio: property management companies. In Arizona, we were lucky enough to find a real estate agency offering everything under one roof. We acquire properties with them, following which they provide us with a detailed report on the costs required to bring the property up to rentable condition. Once we have approved the report, they move ahead with the work. Generally, two weeks later, they choose a tenant. We are serviced with a copy of the lease. Finally, every month, they send us a detailed report on revenue and expenses, along with our monthly check.

Whenever a tenant has a problem, he calls our property management company (not us). As you can see, we are not required to work very hard in this entire process, aside from opening the rent checks they mail to us. **My Secret Number Forty-Two**: have an outstanding real estate team on the ground. A property management company will charge approximately $70 per month per property for their services, which is very reasonable.

Right now, I would like to briefly deal with tax treatment. As you know, rental income and expenses must be included in your annual return. We have done business with a good American accountant since the very beginning. He is very competent and we have complete confidence in him. He was very helpful when we filled out the forms required by the American tax authorities. There is also an agreement between the U.S. and Canada that prevents double taxation. Thus, in paying what we owe to the U.S. and filling out the required form, we do not pay a second time in Canada.

And have no fear when it comes to notaries. We don't need to travel or go anywhere in order to finalize the process of acquiring a property. We can ask our "closing agent" (the equivalent of a notary there) to send us the required paperwork by email. We then sign them and send the documents back by fax. That's all there is to it. On one occasion, we had to send our documents with the original signatures. It's quite rare, but it happens. In that specific case, we used Fedex 24 hour courier service. When choosing your "closing agent" you simply ask your real estate agent to refer you to one. They are generally all competent and governed by laws and a code of conduct as in Canada.

Some people will undoubtedly tell you about complex and expensive legal structures involved in real estate investment in the U.S. If this is your first purchase, I suggest you take care of things yourself and visiting the property personally. Once you've developed a taste for it and consider expanding in this domain, you can move on to an expensive legal structure you find suitable by consulting a tax specialist. The idea is to take things step by step. A final word concerns insurance. Ensure that you are properly covered by a good insurance company with enough civil liability coverage, because as you are no doubt aware, lawsuits happen very quickly in the U.S. The watchword is my **Secret Number Forty-Three**: having adequate insurance coverage is essential. And now, you know our approach to investing in brick and mortar. If you would like to know more about the team we work with on the ground, we invite you to communicate with us. I hope that this chapter has given you a taste for investing seriously in rental property. We are aware that it isn't for everyone. Although it is not the only way to put your money to work effectively, it is one of the best sectors we know.

THE STOCK MARKET

"There are two circumstances in which you should abstain from playing the stock market, the racetrack, baccarat or roulette: first, when you do not have the means, and second, when you do."

Alphonse Allais

French Humorist and Author

You have undoubtedly heard the saying that playing the stock market is a little like gambling. I agree, because the word <u>play</u> applies in both cases. However, "playing" and "investing" are two very different things. Someone who invests in the stock market is really buying businesses, or a fraction of them, while someone who *plays* the stock market is speculating to make a profit or loss in the short term. The market presents a phenomenal amount of wonderful opportunities to build wealth. Many people have lost their shirts in getting involved in it, but some have become very rich. It is an important sector that deserves our consideration, which is why it is included here. I was just 15 when the stock market piqued my curiosity for the first time. We had taken a course on the economy in school and the subject had been briefly covered. I had begun to understand stock market quotes and take an interest in them. A colleague at my weekend job had also become interested in the fascinating world of stocks.

After a brief discussion, he confided that he had a friend who could advise us in business investing. I told him I was interested, and the following week, he had received a tip on a supposedly promising stock. It involved a manufacturing company I had never heard of. Anxious to play the stock market for the first time (please note the word play), I laid down $500 for the stock. I acquired it for $0.39 per share. One month later, the company went bankrupt and I had lost it all. It was a life lesson and my **Secret Number Forty-Four**: never trust a hot tip from your neighbor, because it's almost always ice-cold. Far from being discouraged, I wisely decided to educate myself in-depth by reading a number of books on the stock market. The one I found most memorable, and which remains an inspirational book, is *The Intelligent Investor* by Benjamin Graham.

Graham was born in London and lived there from the early 1900s until 1976. During his career he was recognized as the most gifted investor on the planet. His theory consisted of placing his game pieces on sound investments and holding them over the long term. He described the stock market as a "manic depressive patient." Every day, the market defines action X according to its mood rather than the true value of the company. To invest successfully, Graham teaches us to purchase a blue-chip stock when the "manic-depressive" is depressed and sell it when he is manic. I strongly recommend this book to anyone who wants a better understanding of the machinery and psychology surrounding the stock market. In the '90s, I made some other investments that proved to be more judicious. I believe that being better prepared and informed contributed to my success, but I must admit that those were prosperous years for the market and it was not all that difficult to make money. In all, I had a stock portfolio holding about 10 stocks. However, as a salaried employee at the time, I was limited in how quickly I could progress and acquire stocks, even though all of my savings were directed towards the market.

Towards the end of 1999, I decided to liquidate my investment portfolio. The average return was about 15% compounded annually – not bad for a novice. And I repeat, the '90s were exceptional years for the stock market. I left the market because I was preparing to make the big leap into acquiring my own business, as you already know. Accumulating cash assets had become a priority. Short-term investments were therefore my logical choice.

And it was an advantageous decision. During the '00s on the whole, the stock market delivered a rather disappointing level of return. Some even refer to it as a lost decade. Since then, I've only stepped back into the stock market once, three years back, just before the Federal Reserve in the U.S. decided with a wave of the hand to print up trillions of dollars to rescue the American economy. I decided to invest in precious metals: gold and silver. One ounce of gold was trading under one thousand dollars. Needless to say, investments generated a solid return in little time. Subsequent investments were directed towards companies owning silver mines. An ounce of silver was then about $13, making it another sound choice. It is now 2012, and I am not involved in the market and do not plan to return to it before 2020. There are a number of different stock investor profiles. Some are hyperactive and trade every day ("day traders"). I've never met nor have I heard of anyone who has become rich on a permanent basis by trading in that manner but they may indeed exist. Next, there are the accumulators. These investors constantly make purchases and hold onto their portfolio regardless of events. Then there are those who invest in cycles. This group of investors shows up when opportunities present themselves and retreats when the original conditions change. I am part of this latter group, but am not so presumptuous as to state that you should follow that path. Every investor is different.

There is, however, an industry with which I have a much bigger problem: mutual funds. Many people who do not want to or cannot manage their money themselves place their trust in a mutual fund manager, who takes over managing their capital. That is my **Secret Number Forty-Five**: if you do not want to take care of your money and take charge of it like a ship's captain, someone else will do it. But always in his own interest, and not necessarily in yours. Mutual fund managers loudly proclaim themselves to be the best at selecting winning stocks.

However, less than 25% of them manage to beat the S&P 500 Index!

Even more stunningly, they charge variable management fees that generally fall between 2 and 3 percent, even when they deliver a negative return! Now that is a great business to have! Think about it: being compensated even when they fail to deliver the merchandise. Naturally, they will endlessly tell you that it's only a momentary setback and the market will correct itself. The goal is to keep you in one fund or another in the same family for as long as possible, to rake in the maximum fees. You take on 100% of the risk. They take on 0%. They cash in during good times or bad.

When you're driving along the highway and you spot an attractive billboard featuring a couple enjoying their golden retirement on the beach, bearing the logo of a mutual funds company, remind yourself that it all comes with a cost. They spend at least several thousand dollars every month for this visibility in this one location, and thousands of dollars more to develop the marketing campaign. And where do you think they find that money? In the pockets of those invested in their mutual funds.

That doesn't include their lovely downtown offices with their secretaries and support personnel. All of that chips away further at the return. If you don't wish to manage your money yourself, I suggest that you seek out an Exchange Traded Fund (ETF) that matches the S&P 500 Index, because the management fees are quite low compared to a classic mutual fund. At the very least, you'll match the performance of the Index, which most other managers do not reach. Do you know TV segments I loathe more than anything else? When mutual funds specialists offer their opinions. Invariably, they all say: "You must have sound asset diversification, do not put all your eggs in one basket, and target the long term." The problem is that they repeat the same refrain every time, as though they literally had nothing else to say! It really becomes exasperating over time. The worst of it is that this is not true diversification as far as I'm concerned. From what I have been able to observe, when a correction or a crash hits the market, it hits everywhere, in all sectors. The insurance company and the automobile manufacturer both suffer, although some sectors are impacted somewhat less. I will return later to the issue of what constitutes true asset diversification.

I prefer to invest in market cycles because money does not circulate in a closed system – rather, it involves communicating vessels. When one category appears to have gloomy prospects for the future, money does not disappear, it simply moves towards another more attractive category of assets. One of the factors that prompts this movement is the prevailing interest rate set by our central banks. If you can predict the direction it will move in, you can probably predict which asset categories will be favored.

Right now, in 2012, key interest rates are at their lowest and can only move in one direction: upwards. The question is knowing when. Rising interest rates generally have a negative effect on stock valuations because consumers have less money available for discretionary spending. For their part, businesses are doubly affected, as fewer clients amount to fewer sales and fewer sales generally mean lower profits. Also, businesses must spend additional sums for their new borrowing needs when rates climb. Businesses listed on the stock exchange are evaluated according to their future profits. If the market anticipates a coming drop in profits, the value of the stock will reflect this market anxiety more often than not. The other reason I have left the stock market is my suspicion of what lies hidden in the water beneath the iceberg. And it is not pretty. When the time comes to analyze what the future holds for us, it is important to consider how demographics affect society. Why? Simply put: my parents are 65 and I can safely say that their consumer spending is significantly lower than it was twenty years ago when my brother and I lived at home. Depending on your age, a time comes when you reach the ceiling of your consumer and lifestyle expenses, because your needs evolve with the passage of time. This age is, on average, 56. After this age, your children have generally finished their education and left the family home. As a result, needs and expenses begin to drop year after year.

Unsurprisingly, the largest demographic in our society is represented by the Baby Boomers. Their average age just recently surpassed that critical age of 56. The conclusion to be drawn for the years to come: consumer expenditures slow and with them, likely the economy in general. A decelerating economy is the stock market's worst enemy, and that is why I am so pessimistic about its prospects for at least the next ten years, until another more populous stratum of society takes the reins. But there's more – and it is known as "Japan." As I see it, Japan is a financial catastrophe. In fact it appears to have been bankrupt for some time. Moreover, Greece is a model student right alongside it. At its worst point, Greece had a debt to GDP ratio of 150% (GDP being the sum of all the goods and services created by the country in one year). Generally, a country is considered to be at a crisis point when it surpasses a debt to GDP ratio of 100%. Now get this: Japan is at 250%! The question is no longer whether or not this enormous bubble will burst, but when. And I will predict that they cannot hold on for very much longer. Japan will default on its debt as Greece did. The problem is that Japan has the third largest economy in the world. You surely recall the disruption caused by lightweight Greece, which is dragging down such other vulnerable economies as Italy, Spain, Portugal and Ireland. Now imagine the impact Japan will have on the rest of the planet. It will be a fiscal bomb stamped "Made in Tokyo!"

The reason Japan has been able to continue with its financial Ponzi Scheme this long is that Japan's debt is held by the Japanese themselves. As you know, Japan is the most rapidly aging country on the planet. One of the consequences of aging is that Japan's savings rate is in free-fall. It has gone from double digits during the '80s and '90s when the Japanese were saving up for their old age, to less than 2% of late. Some predict that the Japanese savings rate will be nil within three years. Do you know what that means? The country will no longer be able to finance its current deficit internally. When that happens, do you really believe that international markets will agree to finance their debt at 1% interest, knowing full well that the country is in trouble? When its enormous bubble bursts, that will be the end for Japan.

When that day comes, and rest assured, it will, the impact on global stock markets will be considerable. Some people will probably question my credibility, affirming that Japan is a global industrial power. I respond that Japanese products have taken a hit in recent years, and find it increasingly difficult to compete with other Asian countries.

Here is an example: the major Japanese TV manufacturers are all recording losses as we speak. The situation is quite similar in the automobile sector. They are no longer the undisputed leaders they once were. One need only compare their models with those of other manufacturers to quickly observe how dull they are. Fortunately, they still have their reputation for reliability. However, all the other manufacturers have also made major strides and significant gains in that area over the past few years. Japan is not the only country grappling with an untenable level of debt. In fact, it is a global problem. And there's no help coming as all the economic engines switch off one after another.

Europe is bogged down in a never-ending debt crisis and most of its component countries are in recession. The U.S. is in light recovery mode, but that recovery is fragile. The country's largest problem is its budgetary deficit, which must be solved soon. The cuts to come, along with problems stemming from Europe, will necessarily threaten its rebound. Meanwhile, the big engines of Brazil and India are also out of gas in terms of economic growth. China, supposedly the driving force and superpower that, some say, will dethrone the U.S. in the coming years, is also at a standstill. Their problem is that the country is an exporter. Its two primary markets, the European countries and the U.S., are not in top form – far from it. For that matter, the country's growth figures indicate that it is struggling. The country's best indicator is the one measuring the growth in demand for electrical power. Lately, that demand has stopped rising in China. This leads one to imagine that their economic growth is also nil. Officially, their growth rate is 6.9%, but do not believe it. The Chinese authorities are renowned for being untrustworthy in their official statistics. How is it possible to grow an economy by 6.9% without additional electrical power? There's your answer: it's not. There is no growth. Presently, the central banks in the U.S. and Europe are desperately flooding the markets with cash (trillions of dollars) to keep the entire system from collapsing. However, this is no miracle solution, because they are simply buying time by delaying the inevitable. Furthermore, this has the direct negative effect of artificially inflating global stock markets, greatly increasing the risk of a crash to come. Also, each monetary easing (a clever term that simply means printing money) seems to have a shorter beneficial effect than the previous one.

The next logical step in my opinion is global debt reduction global with massive payment defaults in order to be able to start over on a new sustainable base which more accurately reflects reality. If this scenario materializes, you can be sure that we are heading straight for a depression much more sever than the one experienced in the '30s.

In 2008 during the last financial crisis, our governments missed a great opportunity to allow natural market forces to purge and cleanse the system. Instead, our governments and central banks wanted to restart the engine and piled debt on top of a debt problem. As a result, they put a Band Aid on the wound, and rather than entering the depression we should have experienced, we had a recession which changed nothing about the underlying problem which will lead us towards a far greater crisis. Presently, we are not living under normal market conditions. Market forces are constantly manipulated by central banks injecting trillions of dollars everywhere on the planet. I am wary of anything artificial. My **Secret Number Forty-Six** is: beware anything artificial, because those things are dangerous! I prefer to have an economy built on a solid foundation. What we see happening right now more closely resembles a house of cards ready to collapse at any moment. I will restate: you cannot solve a debt problem with more debt (would you fix a broken leg by breaking it further in the belief that it will heal one day?). That, however, is what our governments and central banks are doing right now.

Sooner or later, we will have to pay the bill, and the longer they live in denial, the worse things will get. Current conditions are so abnormal that I recently decided to increase my liquid holdings. Normally, I do not advise anyone to leave their money sleeping in the bank when they could be investing, for example, in the American real estate market and bringing home 12% in cash flow per year. Once again, conditions are not normal right now.

I don't pretend to be an economist. However, I have good judgment and the ability to look at a situation coolly and see it for what it is. The things I have mentioned in this chapter are not necessarily included in the news. Rest assured that when they finally get around to discussing them, it will be too late, for the sound, simple reason that the entire world will know. News reports on the economy are delivered by specialty journalists describing events that have already taken place, and have therefore already been fully anticipated by the markets. They analyze events by explaining why such and such a thing took place. Their jobs do not involve informing us of what will happen tomorrow. Whenever they attempt to forecast the future, I offer you one piece of advice: turn off the TV and go to bed as though you hadn't heard a word of it. Here's a little list of jargon translations that can be of huge assistance to you when you watch a news report:

"The government is attempting to give the economy a soft landing." Translation: a major crisis and devaluation are underway right now and the government is in panic mode. Moreover, they have no miracle solution.

"This time, things are different." Translation: this phrase has been used umpteen times in history to justify an extravagant and irrational valuation of stocks, sparked by a new technological breakthrough. Example: technology stocks linked to the Internet during the early '00s. As a piece of advice, when you hear that phrase: run! The same phenomenon took place in the past, with the invention of the microprocessor, TV, the telephone, the personal computer, etc... The scenario recurs again and again, and people never seem to learn the lessons of the past.

"We are about to experience peak oil very soon." Translation: we want you to believe in a reality that does not exist by prompting a hike in prices at the pump (and herding the sheep, as they say). Since this theory was offered to the world three years ago, the U.S. beat domestic oil production records this year. Also, a reserve estimated at 40 billion barrels of oil was discovered on Anticosti Island. There was also a similar discovery in Israel! In the meantime, automobile manufacturers have made numerous technological breakthroughs to reduce gas consumption, as well as developing new electric models. The originators of this theory have raked in enormous wealth, at the expense of the masses. In 2008, when the U.S. stumbled, this is what we heard from our TV networks: "The economies of the rest of the world are henceforth uncoupled from the U.S. and will be able to continue their normal growth." Translation:

a theory that belongs in the Stupidity Hall of Fame. The specialists go to great lengths to try to explain their new theory. That's the primary reason why I will never be an "economics expert." The U.S. is the world's largest economy, representing 25% of economic activity on its own. How can an expert with the least bit of intelligence state that normal growth is possible without them? Thanks to China? The major problem is that China is a goods producer. How can China continue to grow if the country's customer is no longer there to purchase its goods? With that, I leave you one of my most valuable secrets, which is **Secret Number Forty-Seven**: do exactly the opposite of what the masses are led to believe and you will have extraordinary results (maintain your own critical attitude).

THE BANK: BOTH ANGEL AND DEMON

"In Monaco, the gangsters don't rob the banks, they own them."

Laurent Ruquier

French TV and radio host

One day, a person bursts into your home and makes the following proposition: he will take your car and rent it out to other people on a daily basis. He reassures you by mentioning that he can return it to you whenever you like upon a simple request from you. However, all revenue will revert to him without you being entitled to it. Does this proposal seem good to you? In fact, you would probably contact the police without a moment's hesitation to report this person before he took advantage of innocent victims. Furthermore, if the police arrested him, they would probably inform him that it isn't really legal to derive income from property that you do not own.

Everyone agrees on this principle. However, this is what the banks do in complete legality, day after day. They manufacture money from nothing, virtually as much as they want. And that's not all – the more money they create and add into the system, the more they depreciate the savings you've earned by the sweat of your brow. They've come up with a lovely word to describe this phenomenon: inflation (when you must spend more to obtain the same product). Many people would consider it completely illegitimate to demand interest on something you do not own, but the banks have laws that protect them.

Have you noticed that the most beautiful skyscrapers downtown are almost all occupied by the banks? And rest assured, those skyscrapers were very expensive. I should also mention the many bank branches spread out just about everywhere across the country, and the thousands of employees at their service. And despite all this, they still generally reap substantial profits. This is not abnormal in and of itself, because they are in business like any other enterprise, to make money. But where does all of this money come from? Have you ever asked yourself that question? I have, because I generally like to know what lies hidden behind the curtain. Did you know that when you deposit your $500 paycheck in the bank, for example, it technically no longer belongs to you? You read that correctly – the $500 belongs to the bank from that moment, and in return, they promise to return it to you if you decide to claim it one day (while charging you withdrawal fees, of course).

Next, the bank is authorized to take its $500 and issue loans up to $5000. This is called the fractional reserve system. In this present case, the ratio is 1 to 10. Now let's create a little scenario together: I show up at the bank and request a loan of $5000 for a trip to Florida with my better half, as we really need to recharge our batteries. The bank has us sign paperwork that commits us to reimburse that amount, plus 12% interest.

Two weeks later, my spouse and I are in tip-top form. However, we have to get back to work quickly because we have made a promise to repay. For an entire year, we get up very early every morning to go to work. Ultimately, after the year in question, it's a done deal: we have successfully repaid our loan. In all, to simplify calculations, let's say this cost us the original amount of $5000 plus $600 in interest. We worked hard during that year and are now ready to go back on holiday on credit!

Now let's take a look at what happened on the bank side of things. With your original deposit of $500, the bank was authorized to issue us a loan of $5000. Thanks to our loan, the bank was able to collect interest revenue of $600. Not a bad return, is it? The bank never contributed a cent of its own money to this affair, but it certainly managed to collect interest revenue of $600 when all is said and done.

My question is the following: you deposited $500 and the bank provided us with $5000 for our trip. So where did they get the other $4500? You will answer, logically, that it comes from other bank depositors, and that's where you go astray. And how! You've got it all wrong. The bank will never lack for money regardless of the number of loan applications it receives. Has the bank ever told you: hang on, let me check if I have enough deposits in my vault to proceed with your loan application? Of course not. Rather, here is what happens: in return for our signature and our promise to repay the amount, the bank simply punched the number $5000 into our bank account using its computer keyboard. Thus, $5000 new dollars were inserted into the system. This is called money creation. The bank turns this magic trick every day. The total of all existing loans makes up the bulk of the money supply, or total dollars, if you prefer. Most people believe that the government manufactures our money. That is true, but only in part, because the Royal Mint is responsible for printing the banknotes and minting the coins. However, that only amounts to 5% of all the money that exists. The balance (95%) is created by banks and financial institutions via loans granted in all their forms (personal loans, lines of credit, credit cards, etc...), and we call this "debt money."

We saw this in the preceding example. The bank created $5000 from nothing by entering that amount into our account. I then spent all that money and kept the economy going, in addition to getting a tan on the beach. Now that you know that the bank is responsible for money creation, you must know that the opposite is also true. Bit by bit, as we repay our loans, that money is destroyed and disappears from the money supply. We can therefore draw the following conclusion: 95% of the money that exists in the world originates from some type of debt. Therefore, without debt, there would be no money, or very little. We have a tendency to mistakenly believe that if everyone were freed of their debts, we would collectively have more money. In fact, the exact opposite is true. That's probably why this subject has never been taught in school. In heady times when everything seems to be going well, the banks loan money hand over fist. The number of loans constantly increases, thereby fattening up the economy as a result. Little by little, the money supply inflates like a big balloon as the bankers pump it full of air. Inflation then makes its appearance, because there are too many dollars in circulation for the amount of products available, sending prices higher. There is, however, a major problem with this. When the bank turns its magic trick, it creates these new dollars via the loans it grants, but it does not create the dollars in interest it demands in return. As a result, there is a permanent lack of dollars in the system, an absence that is impossible to fill. The reality is that the system is doomed to fail from the start. The only way to keep the merry-go-round going is to continually loan more and more to make up the shortfall in the equation.

And then one day, the big bubble bursts. This is what happened in 2008 in the U.S. when the real estate bubble popped. A market event was enough to trigger a domino effect. From one day to the next, the banks turned off the tap and stopped granting loans automatically. This only aggravated the problem. The money supply was in danger of contracting at high speed. The banks, with their inventories of mortgage takeovers, ran the risk of meeting the same fate.

And so the government came to the rescue and picked up the mess. It partly repaired the damage and settled the bill with taxpayers' money. A deep depression had been narrowly averted. However, the rescue mission did not come without consequences for the American budget. Right now, the American national debt is 16 trillion dollars. Before the crisis of 2008, it was under 10 trillion dollars. What does all of this tell you? To me, this indicates that the system is on the verge of caving in. The point of no return seems to have been crossed some time ago. And the only option that remains to them is to continue to go further into debt until, one fine day, the house of cards collapses. I know this is no bed of roses, and I agree. Nonetheless, this is our reality today, and ignoring it changes nothing. One option would be to withdraw the banks' power to create money, returning it fully to governments. However, do you truly believe our friends in the banking world would allow that to happen to them?

The banking cartel is the most powerful force on the planet and no government has experienced any great success in attacking it… with one exception: Iceland. That country succeeded in sending the bank directors who sparked the crisis to prison and nationalizing the country's entire banking system, all while renouncing its obligations to its international creditors. Since then, Iceland is the sole country in the European region to have enjoyed renewed economic growth. It is the only country to have taken such action. It seems that only mass education of the citizenry followed by a popular uprising can change the state of things at the global level. And we are not there. From now until that time, we must realize that we are compelled to experience inflationary periods, when banks even grant loans to people without the means to repay them. That is followed by periods of recession, deflation or depression, when the banks stop approving all loans, even to applicants who are gainfully employed. The problem is that we have not experienced a true depression since the '30s. It's as though we had spent 80 years without living through a winter. We can logically predict that if one ever bursts upon us one day, it will be a doozy! I am not the type of person who wants to revolutionize the current system and change it. In fact, I would rather fully understand how it functions so that I can play my cards right and get out while the getting is good. The best strategy to adopt is **Secret Number Forty-Eight**: I strongly suggest that you avoid consumer borrowing like the plague. Holidays on credit, credit cards, if you cannot pay the entire balance every month. Personal lines of credit, a succession of car loans, borrowing money for more useless cosmetic surgery... I recommend you avoid taking out any of these types of loans because they are guaranteed to impoverish you.

Some people prefer consumption to investing, and I respect their choices. However, if you are among this group, don't go crying to others that you don't have a penny to your name. When you do not have the means to buy something, here are two valid options available to you. First choice: forget the whole thing. Second choice: look for ways to increase your income so that the sought-after article will be within your reach. The worst decision is to request a loan from your banking institution and run into debt for a consumer article that loses value over time. Never forget that the bank is not there for your benefit, it is there for its own. And don't count on the bank to tell you whether or not you have the means equal to your ambitions. The bank will grant your loan application in most cases. Personally, we borrow from our bank only when we can earn money with the loan, which, incidentally, is my **Secret Number Forty-Nine**. Here is an example that demonstrates the concept: we request a loan for our business when the time comes to renovate our locations every ten years. We meet with our banker so that he can approve the entire loan amount required. We use the loan to renovate our business without spending a cent of our own money. That allows us to remain in business and generate operating profits several times higher than the monthly loan payment. And that is how we make money with the bank's money. It is the only instance in which we take out a loan. The same example can apply to real estate. If you borrow a certain amount to purchase a triplex and it provides you with surplus cash flow every month after you have paid your loan and your running costs, you are making money with the bank's money. That is why this chapter is entitled: the Bank, both Angel and Demon, because you are the one who decides, in a sense, whether the bank is an angel or a demon in your life. If you choose to call upon the bank to fulfill your daily consumer desires, it will drag your finances to hell. If, on the other hand, you call upon the bank to make money with its money, it will be the angel on your shoulder and will help you build wealth.

My question to you is as follows: are you the bank's slave, or is the bank at your service? If you have to get up every day and go to work in order to pay your debts and credit cards, you serve the bank and are consequently its slave. The only difference compared to the slavery of 500 years ago is that the chains today are invisible but nonetheless very real and, furthermore, you were the one who chose to bear them. There is one thing that the banks will do everything to avoid. In fact, it is their worst nightmare: the phenomenon known as a bank run. In the last 6 months in Spain, 50 billion Euros have left the country. Spain has been in crisis for three years and experienced the same phenomenon as occurred in the U.S. The country's banks granted massive loans to anyone who wanted to leap into the great real estate bubble. When the crisis exploded in 2008, it hit them as well, signaling that the party was over. Real estate prices collapsed, dragging down thousands of people who could not pay back their loans. People had no choice but to hand the keys back to the bank. There are currently 3 million empty properties in Spain sleeping in the books of Spanish banks, which are almost worthless now. Do the math at about 100,000 Euros apiece and you will come up with a conservative reading of what Spanish banks hold in their balance sheets, considered as assets to be written off (300 billion). That's a hefty bill that will have to be handled by the government, but the amount is so enormous for a country of that size that the government alone cannot bear it all. That's when the European Union intervenes to rescue them with a bailout.

This summary should give you an inkling of the debt crisis striking Europe, and its origins. When people lose confidence in their banking system, they race to withdraw everything they have as soon as possible (a bank run). The problem is that the banks, with their fractional ratio, cannot reimburse all savers at once. Remembers our example from the beginning of this chapter: you had deposited your $500 paycheck and the bank could then proceed and grant me a new loan of $5000 because this complied with the reserve ratio required by the laws in force. If you decide to withdraw $300 from your bank account, the ratio no longer holds and the bank must find the $300 from another depositor to comply with regulations. Now, if a wave of panic sweeps through the country and everyone withdraws their liquid assets at once, we can conclude that the banks can no longer honor their liquidity ratios in relation to the loans they hold in their books. That is precisely when they must be rescued and bailed out. Fortunately, in the case of a bank run, our central banks are there to keep an eye on things and restore confidence – which is the subject of the next chapter.

THE CENTRAL BANKS

"Only the small secrets need to be protected.

The big secrets are protected by public incredulity."

Marshall McLuhan

Author and Philosopher

A country's central bank ranks above the other banks we encounter in our daily lives (called chartered banks). It is, in a sense, the Big Boss. The central bank dictates the key interest rate in force, from which the chartered banks derive their own rates, offering you, in turn, the interest rate on your next mortgage.

Our central banks have the fundamental role of ensuring that the financial system financier of the country is stable and optimal for our economy. When an event arises like the financial crisis of 2008, they react quickly to take action in concert around the world, making billions of inexpensive dollars available to their respective chartered banks. They flood the market with liquidity. If it so happens that the people lose confidence in the system and rush to their chartered banks to withdraw their capital all at once, the chartered banks would have de facto access to billions from their central banks in order to deal with the situation and calm things down. The central bank therefore exists to protect us from that catastrophic scenario. But the question we must ask ourselves is: where does the central bank get these billions?

Simple – the central bank creates them out of nothing. It simply says: here they are. And bingo! Billions of dollars have been created. With one stroke of the keyboard, they can be sent to the chartered banks upon request (but please, do not try this at home!). The bank's other primary weapon is the power to decide to raise or lower the key interest rate. This is called the cost of money. When the system experiences a hike in inflation that becomes difficult to control, the bank tends to raise its rate to contain demand, and lowers it when the economy contracts and heads toward a recession (or a depression). The problem we've experienced over the past four years is that the key interest rate is at rock bottom, and the world's largest economies are all out of gas and experiencing low or zero growth at the same time. Low rates no longer appear to have the expected effect. By the same token, the central banks can no longer really use this tool to further stimulate the economy, since rates are already close to zero. And raising the rate would be even more damaging for households and the economy. In a sense, the banks are caught in a trap at the moment. When a central bank provides billions created from nothing to chartered banks, it charges them very real interest in compensation. The mechanism works like this: let's say the central bank loans one billion dollars to chartered bank A at 1% interest. This very case was just played out recently in Europe: the European central bank advanced 1.2 trillion to chartered banks at 1% interest. Bank A turns around with its billion and buys guaranteed bonds from the government, which bring in 3% interest. Bank A therefore makes a profit of 2% in the operation, in complete security, without any risk. And 2% of one billion is a lot of money for a risk-free operation. You are undoubtedly aware that government bonds are debts that our dear elected officials incur by spending more money than they receive in revenue. That translates into a deficit. And who pays the interest on our government debt? That's right, we do: the taxpayers, with our taxes.

Now let's return to our example. The central bank created 1 billion from nothing and charges 1% interest to Bank A, thereby collecting 1 million in interest per year from the chartered bank. The chartered bank will collect its own 2 million (2%) in profits. Neither one of them spent a cent of its own money in this little operation. The 3 million dollars that they will collectively garner are completely funded by taxpayers – millions of whom get up every morning to go to work and pay that bill. Does that disturb you? I'm sorry, but that is how the system works. In reality, the chartered bank is not content to make just 2% profit as presented in our example. In fact, it has the option to make much more by loaning you this money as a mortgage at 5% (the profit therefore being 4% rather than 2%). Better yet, the bank can loot you for 18% on a credit card! And remember that the bank got this money at just

1% interest. It should also be mentioned that chartered banks do not need the central bank in most cases. In that case, the bank does not have to pay the 1% because it pays nothing in return on our deposits! Now, I sense you're getting hot under the collar. You now understand why I advise you to avoid consumer loans and credit cards with unpaid balances. Don't worry. Whether you live in Canada or elsewhere in the world, central banks generally belong to their respective government. As a result, they belong to us collectively, in a way. The profits they generate are returned to us one way or another. I use the term "generally," because that is not true in the U.S. Their central bank is called the Federal Reserve (also known as the Fed), created on December 23, 1913, and it does not belong to the American government in any way. It is a private bank belonging to a number of privileged individuals. You read that correctly: it is private, and don't bother looking for the names of the people behind this powerful central bank (the most powerful in the world). That is a secret that has been guarded since the Fed was created. You can nonetheless rest assured that if they control the largest central bank in the world, they are therefore the masters of the globe. They are the most influential of people and forces, while remaining invisible and unknown to the public. Ben Bernanke is the current president of the Fed, but in my opinion, his precise title should instead be: public figure representing the Fed.

I am surprised that the American people have never rebelled against this situation, but that's probably because they are mainly unaware of the facts. Some people even maintain that the Federal Reserve contravenes the U.S. Declaration of

Independence and is therefore unconstitutional. For several year now, a very courageous politician in the Republican Party, Ron Paul, has denounced the Federal Reserve and demanded that it simply be abolished. His is certainly a story worth following... but in closing, let me reaffirms that the central banks act independently and are not necessarily accountable to their respective governments. In the case of the Fed, it does not receive a budget, neither from the government nor from Congress. It functions exactly the way a business does, collecting interest revenue on the loans it offers and the securities it buys and sells on the markets. As a case in point, in 2005 it paid 600 million to its shareholders and returned a surplus of 18 billion to the U.S. treasury. At the very least, they were kind enough to return a very large part of it. Now you have a full picture of the banking system. In writing on this subject, I was not trying to denounce it, because it is what it is and has been for a very long time. In fact, this chapter was written to show you chartered banks and central banks as they are, in order to help you understand the system in which we live, but also to help you make better decisions in the future.

Once again, the banks are no different from other businesses, existing to make the most profit possible. From your perspective, you are not obliged to give them any more than necessary.

ASSET ALLOCATION

"If the stock exchange is bad,

close it."

Napoléon Bonaparte

Emperor of France

For some professionals, asset allocation is exclusively a matter for the stock market. They recommend diversification and advise you to be involved in various sectors of financial activity, such as: insurance companies, companies in the manufacturing sector, consumer goods companies, companies in the financial sector... There are many other sectors of activity, but you understand the principle. They select the portfolio by allocating stocks in various categories, then affirm that your risk is balanced and well-distributed. I agree with this kind of thinking, but I suggest above all that you deal in companies that can provide dividends on a regular basis. Dividends represent the share of a company's profits that are redistributed to shareholders on a quarterly basis. I consider dividends to be the equivalent of surplus cash flow in real estate, meaning the money left in your pockets after you have paid all of your expenses. In the chapter on real estate, I suggested that you choose your properties mainly in accordance with that factor, because it is impossible to accurately know in advance what value a property will have in 10 years.

The same principle is true in selecting stocks. It is impossible to know with any certainty what value a stock will have in 10 years. In my opinion, those who choose stocks in terms of the value they think they may obtain in future are essentially speculators. Here is the approach I prefer. For example: Coca Cola is a global corporation present in every country. Let's say that at the day's closing price, the stock provides a dividend yield of 2.7%. We can reasonably predict that the company will be able to pay this dividend again in the years to come. This company has an advantage at the distribution level that its competitors cannot necessarily match. Looking at the price of the stock that day in relation to its earnings, we can see it was trading at 19 times its earnings, which, in any case, is not exactly the bargain of the century.

It is impossible to know what the stock price will be in five years, or even next month. But taking into account the solidity of the stock and its dividend yield, I will possibly invest in it, based on its capacity to pay a similar or even higher dividend in the years to come. All the same, the stock does not seem to be a monumentally great deal. I would therefore probably wait a little until the market was a little more depressed before buying it. I am also very wary of flavor-of-the-month stocks. Apple is a good example. This stock is currently everyone's darling, and my philosophy is: beware anything that makes that much noise. Do you remember Nortel stock 15 years ago? The analysts wouldn't talk about anything else. The stock price was on the Planet Mars and people continued to buy it, simply believing it would climb even higher. This is called speculation, or gambling if you prefer. Apple reminds me a lot of Nortel in terms of the noise it is making on the markets; and even though I am not predicting that Apple will end up going the Nortel route, I do predict that very soon, it will no longer be able to keep up the pace of recent years.

Let us now return to asset allocation. In my opinion, if you really want be diversified, you should not put 100% of your money exclusively in stocks – even if they are distributed in a number of activity sectors. The reason: whether they are in one sector or another, stocks have a tendency to react in the same manner, but to different degrees – in a bull market or bear market alike. During a stock market correction, no stock is truly spared. As I see it, being well-diversified means you also hold investments in rental real estate. In the event of a stock market correction, your real estate assets will not be weakened. Your tenant will continue to pay you his rent as usual, as he needs a roof over his head, regardless of what happens on the stock market.

Now let's continue with diversification. In my view, it is intelligent to have cash assets that are available at all times in case of emergency; or, quite simply if you foresee that a crisis will hit the financial system in several years, and plan to profit from the opportunities that will present themselves. Do not leave your cash assets lying uselessly in a bank account that brings you no return. There are options ensuring that your cash assets bring in a percentage of interest while remaining available at all times. Another form of diversification we use is our business. If you can invest in an existing business, or create one yourself, these are other forms of diversification. At the last few kids parties I attended, I noticed that the person handling the inflatables rentals was in fact a schoolteacher. She had started her own little business over the last few years because she had the entire summer to devote herself to it. That is a perfect form of diversification in terms of revenue sources. My cousin is a fireman, and he just acquired an existing tire sales and installation business. It already had an existing client base, and thanks to his efforts, things are very busy during tire-change season. And he has no problem combining his business with his schedule.

My final source of diversification involves precious metals. We consider this to be our "disaster insurance policy." We have holdings in pure silver coins. Why? Because nobody can invent more gold or silver than actually exists in the ground or has already been extracted. There is an enormous difference between that and banknotes, which can be printed up ad infinitum. If the financial system collapses one day, we will all want to have something other than a worthless paper banknote. If that day ever materializes, the value of gold and silver will reclaim the prized position they have held throughout human history. In Zimbabwe in 2008, the central bank increased the money supply (Zimbabwean dollars) to such an extent that the country's inflation rate reached a record 100,000%. By the end, banknotes were in billion-dollar denominations. Their money was worthless and was subsequently abandoned in 2009. The American dollar has since been adopted. I'm not saying that this catastrophic scenario will happen to us, because nobody can predict such a thing. As you may have noticed, nobody buys an insurance policy for their home in the hopes that it will burn down. They take out the policy in the slim possibility that it might happen one day. That's the same principle that led us to procurer silver bullions. History is a great teacher – and it reveals that the value of one asset category can take on proportions that run contrary to all reason. The gold medal-winning event was Holland's Tulip Mania financial rampage in the 1630s. Speculation in the bulbs was so rampant that, according to a story, a house was traded for 3 tulips in 1633! Even immortal painter Rembrandt was taken in by the speculation movement. And so, as you can see, speculation can blind   people   to   reality.

A LITTLE PAUSE

"Whenever you find yourself on the side of the majority, it is time to pause and reflect."

Samuel Langhorne Clemens

Author and Humorist

Now that we are done with the chapters on the financial system and asset allocation, it's time to take a little break and look at things from a broad perspective. You have no doubt remarked that we are right in the middle of a period of economic turbulence. That observation is confirmed by the fact that practically every country in the world is currently experiencing an unprecedented state of crisis, with debt levels that are quite simply untenable. In my opinion, some time between now and 2015, we will experience a crisis of previously unseen magnitude, thereby forcing the system, the people, businesses and governments to reduce their debt. That is the only way we can get things going again on a more solid foundation. This crisis will sweep away a large amount of unprepared businesses and individuals. Those who will make it through with flying colors will be those individuals and businesses who carry the least debt and best control their costs. This is why I mentioned that we currently hold an abnormally high level of liquidity, because we are living through an abnormal period. We want to be prepared for the worst, but also to take advantage of the incredible opportunities that will present themselves along the way. Every crisis brings with it a raft of opportunities seldom seen in a lifetime.

There are two plausible scenarios for the coming years:

Scenario One: Our leaders continue to live in complete denial and we continue to indebt ourselves further. A new word may come into use. Instead of speaking of debt in trillions (one thousand billion) we may speak of *one thousand* trillion. Imagine a news report in 2020 informing us: Today, ladies and gentlemen, the U.S. has surpassed the threshold of 20,000 trillion in accumulated debt, and Congress will have to approve raising the debt ceiling!

In this scenario, inflation would be on the menu for years to come. I believe that is very plausible, because it is what we have done since World War II up until the present day. I remember when Reagan was in power during the '80s and the nuclear arms race was in full swing. The U.S. ran a large budget deficit. Many experts predicted it would end, proclaiming in the Op-Ed pages that the country could not continue along the same course. Twenty years later, as we scan the tableau of their accumulated debt, it must be noted that they continued on the same path.

Scenario Two: there is a market event that spurs a domino-effect crisis. The world's governments intervene collaboratively, but the crisis is out of control. Their efforts are useless or have a short-term effect. In this scenario, a depression would materialize, with a generalized drop in prices. The enormous global debt bubble would simultaneously explode. The damage to business and private individuals would be huge. Bankruptcies would number in the millions.

On the other hand, it would allow for a clean sweep, crossing out a lot of bad debts. That would force all individuals, businesses and governments to massively reduce their debt. No one can precisely predict which scenario will arise. However, there is also a scenario between those two: a reality check and deficit reduction followed by a period of economic stagnation, with neither pronounced economic growth nor downturn. Preparing for the worst seems to be an intelligent choice. As people like to say, an ounce of prevention is worth a pound of cure – even financially.

WHAT'S ON THE MENU?

"The American people's expectations are that we will fail.

Our mission is to exceed their expectations."

George W. Bush

President of the United States of America

I now pose this question to you: what's on the menu for your life in the years to come? Has this book brought you any new ideas, or new ways of thinking? I have offered you all of my secrets because they were truly beneficial to us and made all the difference in our lives. The choice is now yours, whether to apply them in your life, or leave them on the shelf and continue your daily grind as it was before you turned the first page.

When I go to a restaurant, I like to see a wide range of choice on my menu, not just spaghetti with meat sauce. Here is my hope for your menu: diversify it to make it interesting. Having a job is gratifying, but other great projects can also be undertaken even though that may seem unrealistic at first glance. Above all, do not tell yourself: it's too late, because we already have children and cannot take any risks. Nobody is asking you to ditch your job tomorrow morning. You can always engage in small projects and experiences without dropping everything else. I am sure that there are still some dreams close to your heart that you have yet to accomplish. Don't worry, I haven't accomplished all of mine either. If I had, my "bucket list" would be 100% complete.

If you need a mentor to motivate yourself, feel free to contact us. It would be our pleasure to accompany you in the quest to achieve the kind of life you choose. I know that the mountain may seem very high and steep before you reach the summit. My **Secret Number Fifty**: reaching the summit involves taking one step after another, without thinking too much about the effort required nor the total height, while still keeping the ultimate goal in mind.

That's where I am right now – the same place you are. Do you recall that, at the beginning of the book, I wrote that you had to foresee the next stage once you had accomplished your goals? I have accomplished my original goals, which were to become wealthy and have a successful business. The next chapters in my story are posted on a big cardboard sign prominently displayed in my office. That's my Life Plan for what is to come in the next twenty years. Two years ago, I entertained myself by forecasting the next stages in this wonderful adventure. In these outlines, I will share my expectations with you:

I am on the verge of accomplishing two of the goals:

-Write a book by 2015

-Own a colonial home down south

The others are:

- Create two new online businesses by 2018

- Acquire three new businesses by 2020

- Create a hotel chain

- Own 1000 real estate properties by 2025

- Have one of our companies listed on the stock exchange by 2030

- Organize a millionaires' cruise in the Caribbean

- Become a global speaker by 2020

- Develop a trademark by 2025

- Own a private jet by 2032

Now it's your turn to create your future and try your hand at this exercise. Plan out your own road ahead and fill it with your wildest dreams. Once you've completed this stage, you will realize that your mountain is as high as mine. And so, in a way, we are both starting out from the same stage. All that now remains is that we encourage one another to put one foot in front of the other. Next thing we know, we'll be at the summit one day, without having realized how gradual the climb has been.

And so I wish us both the best of luck. Always remember that life is not meant to be boring, that you should enjoy it and fulfill yourself. Thank you for having invested this time in your future development. I appreciate the distance we have traveled together during the course of this book and hope you have enjoyed it as well. And so now, in the hope that our paths will cross one day, I will simply sign off by saying: see you soon!

For more information about Dany Tremblay upcoming 2015 book: Billionaire right next door please visit us at:

www.billionairerightnextdoor.com

ACKNOWLEDGEMENTS

I would like to begin by thanking my publisher, Alain Williamson, for giving me a tremendous opportunity in allowing me to join forces with him and his wonderful team.

Enormous thanks to Chantal for her patience, which was sometimes put to the test during the writing of this book...

Thanks to my parents, who were my first readers and who encouraged me to press on. Thanks to my mother, who poured many hours into revisions and corrections.

And thanks to my management team and my employees, who dedicate themselves and their work to my business every day. I love every one of you... And finally thanks to you.

THE AUTHOR

Dany Tremblay was born into a modest middle class family, a close-knit clan that nonetheless experienced its share of trials and tribulations over the years, as many do. After completing a specialized study program and working in his field of study for five years, he discovered at the young age of 25 that his true future lay elsewhere. For over 12 years, he has run a business with his spouse that generates a multi-million dollar turnover and employs over 100 people.

He happily shares the stories of his investments here, both good and bad, which in just a few years ultimately propelled him to a level of success he could only have dreamt about. For more information's about our products and the new book of Dany Tremblay: Billionaire right next door (release in the beginning of 2015) you can visit us at:

www.billionairerightnextdoor.com

www.ingramcontent.com/pod-product-compliance
Lightning Source LLC
Chambersburg PA
CBHW060240050426
42448CB00009B/1538